© 2000 Mandragora. All rights reserved.

La Mandragora s.r.l.
piazza Duomo 9, 50122 Firenze
www.mandragora.it

Text: Carlo Montrésor
Editing and captions: Andrea Paoletti, Monica Fintoni
English translation: Mark Roberts
Graphic design: Andrea Paoletti, Franco Casini

Photographs: Nicolò Orsi Battaglini, Archivio dell'Opera di Santa Maria del Fiore,
Opificio delle Pietre Dure, Franco Casini, Archivio Mandragora

Printed in Italy

The Opera del Duomo Museum in Florence

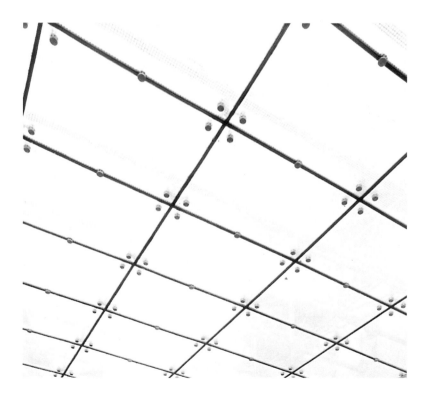

Mandragora

Anna Mitrano

President of the Opera
di Santa Maria del Fiore

The Museum of the Opera di Santa Maria del Fiore was inaugurated on 3 May 1891. After more than a century without any substantial alterations, its structures were in need of modernisation. The administration of the Opera took the occasion of the Jubilee of 2000 to renovate all the rooms housing the famous masterpieces from the monumental complex consisting of the Cathedral of Santa Maria del Fiore, the Baptistery of San Giovanni and Giotto's Campanile. Plans were drawn up by the architect Luigi Zangheri, assisted by the architect David Palterer. The new arrangement was designed, under the supervision of Professor Antonio Paolucci and Monsignor Timothy Verdon, by Dr Francesca Petrucci. Work began in October 1988 and was finished in December 1999. On 23 December the Museum was inaugurated in the presence of the civic and ecclesiastical authorities, and on 29 December it opened its doors to the public.

A great many alterations have been carried out on the Museum's building, the palazzo where Brunelleschi, Donatello and Michelangelo worked. We have sought to guarantee for the works displayed the best possible conservational conditions: new heating and air-conditioning ensures a constant year-round temperature inside the Museum, and all the rooms are protected by a modern video surveillance system. But above all we have tried to meet the needs of the public: throughout the Museum architectural barriers have been removed, new lighting has been installed, and the visitors' route has been rationalised according to criteria of provenance. The exhibits are accurately labelled, in Italian and English, so that visitors can find their way without difficulty and can fully appreciate the Museum's collection. The covering of the courtyard has considerably extended the display space, and on the top floor a room has been equipped as an educational centre for lectures and conferences. There are facilities for non-sighted visitors. Finally the Opera has organised language and art history courses for its staff, so that visitors may receive qualified assistance.

The new rearrangement is however only a first stage in the general reorganisation of the display areas, planned for the near future thanks to the acquisition of the 18th-century Teatro degli Intrepidi, adjacent to the Museum.

It is my hope that the Opera's efforts to make its Museum more welcoming and functional will continue to delight visitors from Florence and from all over the world.

Florence, 8 September 2000

Opposite, a view of the Florentine cathedral complex: the Baptistery of San Giovanni (foreground), the Cathedral of Santa Maria del Fiore with its 19th-century façade and Brunelleschi's dome, and Giotto's Campanile (on the right). Below, right, CODEX RUSTICI, *Santa Maria del Fiore* (mid-15th century), detail (Seminario Maggiore del Cestello): on the page showing the Cathedral, we can clearly see the façade begun by Arnolfo di Cambio, and the marble revetment of the sides and apse. The codex takes its name from the Florentine goldsmith Marco di Bartolomeo Rustici, who dictated the text to an amanuensis and illustrated it with his own drawings in brown ink and water-colour (1447-1448 and 1451-1453) on his return from a voyage to the Holy Land (1441-1442). What we know about him comes from documents published by Ugo Procacci in 1955: in 1427 he shared a workshop with Dino del Monte; he worked for the friars of Santissima Annunziata, where he intended to build a chapel, and for the nuns of Santa Felìcita (in the Oltrarno) who commissioned from him four candlesticks of gilded and enamelled copper. The pen-and-ink drawings illustrating a vernacular version of St Augustine's *De civitate Dei* are attributed to him, as well as the codex which bears his name. The Codex Rustici is divided into three books: the first (fols. 1r-80v) deals with Florence, the second (fols. 80v-167r) and third (fols. 167v-281v) with the goldsmith's journey and the various stages of the pilgrimage, ending with a eulogy of Florence. Owned by the Vignali family, it was stolen in the early 19th century. Subsequently recovered, it has been in the library of the Seminario Maggiore del Cestello, Florence, since 1813. As well as several scenes and drawings of plants and animals it contains, in the first book, representations of thirty-seven Florentine churches and their respective titular saints.

The Opera and its museum

The Opera del Duomo Museum takes its name from an institution which has recently celebrated its 700th anniversary: it began life immediately after the foundation of the Cathedral of Santa Maria del Fiore, whose first stone was laid on 8 September 1296.

In the Middle Ages the construction of a great religious building required the labours of several generations. For us moderns, the idea of beginning to build something that we should never live to see completed would be frustrating in the extreme. Indeed, only deep religious faith and an overwhelming sense of belonging to a society were capable of driving its members to undertake such vast projects to the glory of God and of the civic community.

However highly motivated the builders of the Cathedral were, the economic and organisational difficulties they faced were such as could only be overcome by close collaboration between the republican government and the citizenry. The Opera del Duomo, a municipal institution with the rank of a magistrature, was entrusted with overall responsibility for the new cathedral, including the delicate matters of supervising the design and the construction, and of choosing the architect and the artists who would carry out the sculptural and pictorial decoration. For its part, the Republic undertook to finance the greater part of the work from taxation; in addition, it assigned to the Opera in perpetuity the revenue from the forests of the Casentino, high up the valley of the Arno. The trunks of trees felled in these forests were a valuable commodity: floated down river to Florence and beyond, as far as the sea, they were used in the ship-yards of the Tyrrhenian coast.

Any remaining costs were borne by the generosity of individuals and especially of the guilds. These powerful corporations, which effectively ran the city's economy, collaborated closely with the Opera during its first thirty years of life. There were serious difficulties in co-ordinating the guilds, however, and in 1331 patronage of the Cathedral was assumed exclusively by the Arte della Lana or Wool Guild, whose symbol, the *Agnus Dei* or Lamb of God, became the device of the Opera. It was not until 1770 – when the ruling house of Habsburg-Lorraine, the successors to the Medici, suppressed the guilds altogether – that this close relationship came finally to an end.

Above, the symbol of the Arte di Calimala (an eagle clutching a bale of wool in its talons) on a pilaster on the east side of the Baptistery, whose patronage was held by the merchants' guild. Below, the *Agnus Dei*, symbol of the Arte della Lana, on the west wall of the Palazzo of that name (the headquarters of the Arte since 1308). Right: CIRCLE OF BERNARDO DADDI, *Madonna of Mercy* (1342), detail of fresco (Museum of the Bigallo). The extraordinary cityscape at the feet of the Virgin has been described as the "first attempt known to us to show the city in its entirety" (Fanelli) and may well be the earliest known image of 14th-century Florence: encircled with walls, bristling with towers, dominated by the Baptistery. The picture documents in realistic fashion the numerous buildings under construction at the time: the façade of the Cathedral interrupted at about half its height, the new Campanile still being built, and, behind, the Romanesque basilica of Santa Reparata, by now "small in comparison with so great a city" (Villani), gradually incorporated into the new cathedral.

One might think that once the dome had been completed – its constructional problems having been solved, after years of heated discussion, by the genius of Filippo Brunelleschi – the by-then hundred-year-old institution would have little else to do; but this was far from being the case, for many good reasons.

For one thing, there was the matter of the façade. Designed at the end of the 13th century by the cathedral's first architect, Arnolfo di Cambio, and only completed in its lower portion, it had come to seem impossibly outdated by the time of the Renaissance, and was removed in 1587. (The façade did not receive its present appearance until 1871, when the neo-gothic design by the architect Emilio De Fabris was chosen.) Secondly, the huge church – exceeded in size only by San Pietro in Rome, St Paul's in London and the Cathedral of Milan – required constant and careful maintenance. Thirdly, changes in taste and the ever-present desire to enrich the interior with new works of art made the existence of a decision-making regulatory body essential.

Above, DOMENICO DI MICHELINO, *Dante and his poem* (1465), detail, tempera on canvas (Cathedral of Santa Maria del Fiore). Despite its symbolic character, the view of Florence on the right faithfully records several contemporary features: the drum of the dome is still lacking its marble revetment, and Andrea del Verrocchio's gilded bronze globe is not yet in place on the lantern. The painting – Florence's posthumous attempt to make up for her ungrateful treatment of her greatest poet, who died in exile – was commissioned from Domenico di Michelino by the Opera del Duomo in January 1465. After only five months the painters Neri di Bicci and Alesso Baldovinetti were asked to assess it; they were so satisfied that they recommended for Domenico a higher fee than the one stipulated in the contract. Right, a view of Brunelleschi's dome in a drawing by LUDOVICO CIGOLI (16th century), now in the Gabinetto Disegni e Stampe degli Uffizi: at upper left, the section of the Florentine dome is compared to those of St Peter's and of the Pantheon, in Rome.

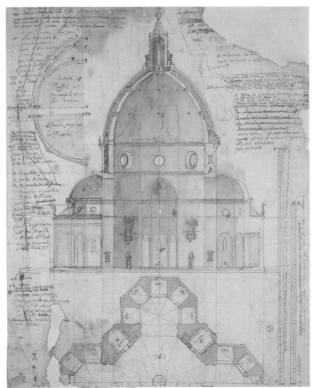

Below, MICHELANGELO's *David*. In 1461 the Operai had entrusted a block of marble to Agostino di Duccio so that he could make a gigantic statue, but the project came to nothing. The marble was passed from one sculptor to another and became so ruined that, as Vasari wrote, "the Operai of Santa Maria del Fiore… without troubling to finish it, had simply abandoned it, and thus it remained for many years". In 1501 it was given to the young Michelangelo, who began to work on it in the Palazzo dell'Opera, building a screen around it so that no-one could see what he was up to. When it was finished it was much discussed by the committee (which included Botticelli and Leonardo), and eventually a location was chosen for it outside the Palazzo Vecchio. It remained there for over three centuries, until it was moved in 1873 to the Accademia. The tribune which still houses it, as within a deliberately 'sacred' space, was designed by Emilio De Fabris, the architect responsible for the 19th-century neo-gothic façade of the Cathedral (→ pp. 166-169).

In 1432, only four years before the completion of the dome, the members of the Opera commissioned from Brunelleschi a new and, as we should say today, 'multi-purpose' headquarters: as well as housing the Opera's offices, the new building would have to contain all the works removed from the Cathedral because considered, rightly or wrongly, inadequate to its increasing splendour. In addition, sculptors and stonecutters would have to be able to work in a courtyard surrounded by a loggia (this space, where Michelangelo carved his celebrated *David*, would disappear in the course of the 19th-century reconstruction).

The present headquarters of the Opera looks very different from the original one. The first major reconstruction took place in the late 1880s, when in the year after the fifth centenary of the birth of Donatello (1887) it was decided to reassemble the *disiecta membra* of his Cantoria and of Luca della Robbia's, both of which had been removed from the Cathedral some two hundred years previously, and to exhibit these two masterpieces side by side. This project, which transformed the headquarters of the Opera into an art museum, was promoted by the architect Luigi Del Moro. He presented his plan in 1885, and it was put into practice in 1891: in many ways it represents the point of departure for the modern art-historical study of the Cathedral/Baptistery/Campanile complex.

Over the course of centuries many pieces of sculpture and architectural fragments had become dispersed: some statues were in the gardens of private Florentine houses, others had found their way into various public collections, and others again were languishing in the deposits; the situation of the paintings was no better, and even today a number of pictures still cannot be traced. The first works transferred to the new museum were the two cantorie, which until 1688 had stood above the doors of the two sacristies in the Cathedral, and which had provisionally been housed in the Uffizi gallery. They were followed by many other works of art, which in the 1940s and 1950s necessitated additional restructuring of the rooms. With the emergence of the serious problem of damage caused to open-air sculpture by atmospheric pollution – the result of heavy and inadequately-regulated traffic – statues and panels were removed from the Campanile and added to the collection in the Museum, their places being taken by copies.

"The foundation was laid with great solemnity on the Nativity of St Mary [8 September], in the presence of the pope's Cardinal Legate and several Bishops, and there was the Podestà and the Captain and the Priors, and all the Orders of the Signoria of Florence, and it was consecrated to St Mary under the name of Santa Maria del Fiore": thus Giovanni Villani recorded in his *Chronicle* the ceremony of the laying of the first stone (1296). The people however "had difficulty in giving up the old name" (Richa): a decree of 1412 invites the citizens to make use of the new name rather than calling it Santa Reparata. The miniature (above) by FRANCESCO D'ANTONIO DEL CHIERICO (*Edili* 151, fol. 7v) shows the consecration of the Cathedral, which took place on 25 March 1436. In the foreground are Pope Eugenius IV and Cardinal Giuliano degli Orsini (holding the cross); at the sides of the doorway, two niches with statues (possibly the two *Evangelists* by Nanni di Banco and Donatello, → pp. 34-39). The procession made its way from Santa Maria Novella on a wooden bridge specially made for the occasion; once inside the church, the priests found themselves beneath the almost completed dome – work would be finished in August, though the lantern would still be missing for a while.

The disastrous flood of 1966, when the collection on the ground floor was submerged to a height of two metres, did not put an end to the work of scholars, nor to the acquisition and cataloguing of new pieces; in fact in a certain sense the disaster acted as a stimulus, and – as in many other departments of Florentine life – was an incentive to further achievement.

The most important event of the last half-century is however the radical restructuring and reorganising which began early in 1999 and at the time of writing (June 2000) is still not completely finished: hence, incidentally, the occasional gaps which the visitor may encounter in the present guide. A series of services have been installed (heating, lifts, lavatories, new lighting), greatly increasing the comfort and manageability of the Museum. The courtyard, which one has to cross in order to reach the interior, has been covered over by a large sky-light, or rather by a transparent ceiling, so as to form an attractive display area. The original implements used for the construction and maintenance of the dome, and the wooden models for Brunelleschi's masterpiece, which used to be displayed in two rooms on the ground floor, have been moved to new and larger spaces, where there is also a collection of the designs made in various periods for the façade of the Cathedral. It has also been possible to recover from the deposits of the Opera a number of pieces of great art-historical interest, and to find a better location for others (such as the surviving sculptural fragments by Tino di Camaino, formerly placed on brackets beside the stairs between the mezzanine and the first floor).

We must not conclude this brief introduction without a glance to the future. The most pressing need is undoubtedly to find a home not only for those works already in restoration, but also for the ones still exposed outside. Spectacular as it is, the intervention on the Door of Paradise – which will be completed within a few years, allowing all the panels to be remounted onto the restored frames – should not be allowed to overshadow the condition of the other two bronze doors of the Baptistery, and of the remaining stone sculpture decorating the cathedral doors. A very considerable financial and organisational effort will have to be made, and the Opera will have to rely on assistance both from the State and from private sponsors.

In 1999 there was a further development with important implications for the future: the purchase of an extensive property just next to the Museum. At one time the Theatre of the Intrepidi, this large space (about 1,000 square metres) has until now been used as a garage. When it has been suitably restored it will not only be able to house the works we have mentioned but will also provide a new home for some of the masterpieces – such as Michelangelo's *Bandini Pietà* – now displayed in far from ideal conditions.

So there is a great work in progress at the Museum, where tradition and innovation coexist in constant synergy. For example, few other museums in the world can boast both a cast-gallery and a working sculptors' atelier, where the heirs of the Opera's stonecutters make copies and restore antique pieces. Visitors can see for themselves this sculptural workshop, in the nearby Via dello Studio, looking exactly like a *bottega* of the Florentine Renaissance. The members of the Opera draw upon the youngest and most innovative talent in the city, to safeguard the artistic patrimony gathered by their remote predecessors.

Above, Nanni di Banco, *Sculptor and Stonecutter* (1416), details from the famous bas-relief of the tabernacle of the Arte dei Maestri di Pietra e Legname, known as the Tabernacle of the *Four Crowned Saints* (Orsanmichele, north side, first order; there is a copy at Via dello Studio 23r, the workshop of the Opera). Among the tools most used by sculptors and stonecutters was the *picchiarello* (above, held by the sculptor), a small pickaxe introduced into Italy in the early 14th century and used for detailed work on stone, especially useful with hard materials or with not very friable calcareous stone; and the drill, held almost perpendicular to the surface to make holes and grooves of uniform size (below, held by the stonecutter). These tools are also shown in the famous hexagonal panel representing *Sculpture* (→ p. 87) from the lower order of Giotto's Campanile. Right, the new covered courtyard – Brunelleschi's dome is visible through the transparent ceiling.

On the façade of the Museum, a marble plaque commemorates Cesare Guasti (1822-1889), author of *Santa Maria del Fiore* (1887), an invaluable collection of documents, most of them unknown at the time, discovered by Guasti in the archives of the Opera di Santa Maria del Fiore. The critical selection, transcriptions and commentary are prefaced by an analytical discourse in which Guasti reconstructs the various stages in the construction of the Cathedral and Campanile. Below, bust of Grand Duke Cosimo I de' Medici (1519-1574) by the sculptor GIOVANNI BANDINI.

1. The exterior

The simple exterior reflects the process of 'normalisation' typical of many Florentine buildings. Between the 15th and the 17th century numerous medieval tower-houses and small dwellings, built back to back to each other and often belonging to a single family, were incorporated together behind façades built in accordance with the principles of renaissance architecture.

To accommodate its new headquarters the Opera had purchased a number of houses from the Falconieri family: their coat of arms (a ladder with three rungs) can still be seen between the first and second arches on the left of the façade, attesting to the survival beneath the plaster of the original external wall. On the opposite side is the *Agnus Dei*, symbol of the Opera. Above the doorway is a BUST OF COSIMO I, by Giovanni Bandini: it was set up in 1572, a year after the establishment of the Medici Grand Dukedom. Around the niche containing this bust runs the inscription COSMVS MEDICES MAGNVS D(ux) ETRVRIÆ ("Cosimo de' Medici, Grand Duke of Tuscany"); above, two cherubs support the Grand Ducal coronet, on the fascia of which another inscription records the concession of the title by Pope St Pius V. At the lower border of the oval a lion's head bears the insignia of the Order of the Golden Fleece, the highest knightly order of the Holy Roman Empire.

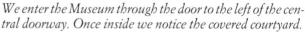

The sides of the Etruscan cippus (first half of the 5th century BC) are decorated with groups of three figures: the one shown to the right represents a *flute-player between two men*; the other two have a woman between two dancing men (one of them is stroking her chin), and a lyre-player between two figures. The double flute (*aulós*) and the lyre (*kitharís*) were the most widely played instruments in the Greek world, which later exported them to other cultures: they were played by soloists or employed to accompany recitation and song.

We enter the Museum through the door to the left of the central doorway. Once inside we notice the covered courtyard.

2. The entrance

As soon as we have passed the ticket counter we find on our right the upper portion of a marble ETRUSCAN CIPPUS of 1 the first half of the 5th century BC, showing musicians and dancers. This fragment, probably brought to Florence as a curiosity by some learned canon of the Cathedral, possibly comes from Chiusi (the ancient *Clusium*), and was rediscovered in the 19th century in the cellar of the house belonging to the cathedral clergy.

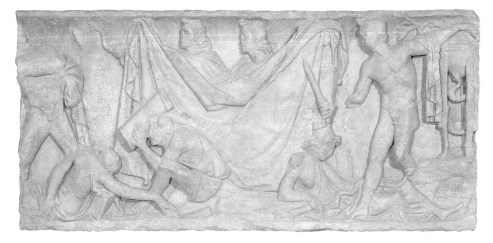

Above, sarcophagus front with the myth of Orestes (2nd century AD): on the right, the hero grasps a sword and approaches the sacred tripod of Apollo, from whom he hopes to find refuge from the pursuing Erinyes, portrayed with serpents. Below, the front of a cinerary urn (2nd century AD).

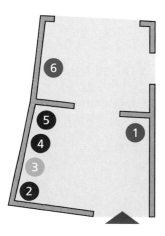

Set deeply into the left wall are marble fragments of Imperial Roman funerary art: they were at one time incorporated into the structures of the Campanile and of the Cathedral, and they demonstrate how extensive were the remains of Roman Florentia in the Middle Ages. The piece at lower left, and the central one, are FRAGMENTS OF SAR- 2, 4 COPHAGI with cupids and date from the 3rd century AD. To the right there is a slightly earlier SARCOPHAGUS FRONT 5 (mid-2nd century AD); damaged on the left side, it shows the Greek myth of Orestes. The hero, having taken revenge on his mother Clytaemestra – who with her lover Aegistus had butchered her husband Agamemnon on his return from Troy – is being pursued by the Erinyes. This fragment was removed in 1877 from the corner between the façade and the north side of the Cathedral.

The fragment at upper left is the FRONT OF A CINERARY URN 3 (2nd century AD), reminding us that the practice of cremation coexisted in the Roman world with that of burial.

At the end of the corridor, on the left, there is a FRAGMENT 6 OF A MEDALLION from the workshop of Arnolfo di Cambio, showing the head of a putto; it dates from the early 14th century and was part of the original decoration on the façade of the Cathedral.

Turning to our right we now enter the first room. As we go through the doorway we notice two facing inscriptions commemorating the recent restructuring of the Museum, one with the monogram of the Opera, 'OPA' (where the barred 'p' is the abbreviation for 'per'), the other with the date A.D. MM ("the year of the Lord 2000").

Around 1320 the Sienese TINO DI CAMAINO made three sculptural groups, which were placed above the three doors of the Baptistery; after almost two centuries the gothic statues seemed "clumsy and worn", and it was decided to replace them. Of the group placed over the East door (*The Baptist with the Theological Virtues*) remain today only *Faith* and *Charity* (right) and *Hope* (opposite). Tino's statues were replaced by Sansovino's *Baptism of Christ* (→ pp. 179-181), now also in the Museum; the Theological Virtues 'survived' on the base of the *Beheading of the Baptist* (1569-1570), sculpted by Vincenzo Danti for the South door. Born in Siena around 1285, Tino was master of the cathedral works at Pisa (1315) and then at Siena, where he was forced to return after fighting alongside the Guelfs against the Pisans. He was later in Florence, where he made the tomb of the bishop Antonio d'Orso inside the Cathedral, and in Naples, where from 1322 until his death he worked for Robert of Anjou. He is best known for his many funerary monuments, characterised by a rounded style influenced by Arnolfo di Cambio, and somewhat reminiscent of Sienese painting.

3. The Room of Tino di Camaino

In this small room are displayed the surviving fragments from sculptural groups by the Sienese artist Tino di Camaino which between 1320 and 1321 were set up above the Baptistery doors, where they remained until the early 16th century.

Beneath the windows are marble busts of the three Virtues which decorated the east door of the Baptistery, facing the Cathedral: from the left we see HOPE (crowned with ivy), FAITH (wearing a crown) and CHARITY (holding the cornucopia). The identification of the third bust is uncertain; it may be a Sibyl, and in that case Charity could be the group now to be seen in the Bardini Museum.   1-3

Right and on the opposite page,
TINO DI CAMAINO, bust of the
Redeemer in Benediction and head
of the *Baptist* (ca. 1320-1321).
In the 16th century the new group
representing the *Baptism of Christ*,
"the essential component in the
iconographic cycle of the Baptist"
(Giusti), was set up over the East
door → pp. 179-181); to the South
door was assigned Danti's group
of the *Beheading of the Baptist*, a
subject not attempted by Tino.
Below, a detail of a 15th-century
nuptial *cassone* ('chest') now in the
Bargello: attributed to GIOVANNI
TOSCANI, it shows the procession of
the *palii*, the decorated banners
which were offered in the Baptistery
on the feasts of St John the Baptist,
patron saint of Florence: Tino's
sculptures can be seen in a gothic
aedicule, cusped and tripartite.
At lower right we see the original
location of the 14th-century groups
by Tino, and of the 16th-century
groups which replaced them.

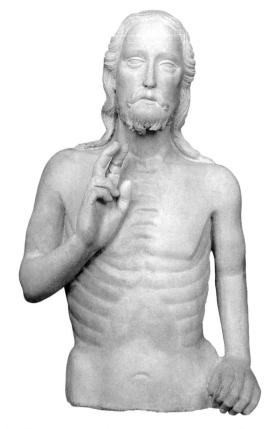

On the wall opposite the entrance are two fragments
from the south door of the Baptistery. Of the group by
Tino – showing St John in the act of baptising Christ,
whose clothes were supported by an angel – there remain
only the BUST OF THE REDEEMER IN BENEDICTION (left) and the   4
HEAD OF THE BAPTIST (right).   5

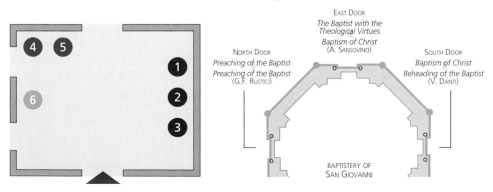

Above, TINO DI CAMAINO, head of the *Baptist* (ca. 1320-1321): this superb fragment is all that remains of a group that once stood above the North door. In 1506 the Consuls of the Calimala decided to retain the iconographic theme of Tino's group (the *Preaching of the Baptist*) and commissioned a group of the same subject from GIOVAN FRANCESCO RUSTICI (above, right). Giorgio Vasari, who discerned in the new figures "grace and terrible bravura", may well have been correct in stating that the sculptor was assisted by Leonardo da Vinci, who like Rustici had been trained in the workshop of Andrea del Verrocchio: the head of the Levite on the right ("a plump pumpkin which is most beautiful" – Vasari) is in fact somewhat Leonardesque.

On the wall to the left of the entrance, between the two arches leading into the next room, we see another HEAD OF 6 THE BAPTIST, all that remains of a group that once stood above the north door. The subject represented by Tino (*The Baptist preaching to a Pharisee and a Levite*) would be taken up almost two centuries later (1506-1511) by Giovan Francesco Rustici, whose own group is now to be seen above the north door.

We now enter the small passage leading to the Room of the Old Façade.

4. The passage

On the left wall and on the wall opposite the entrance there are three sculptures from the door on the south side of the Cathedral known as the *Porta del Campanile*.

In the centre, inside the lunette, stood the MADONNA 1 AND CHILD (1379-1380), attributed to Simone di France-

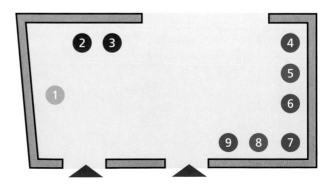

Exposed to the elements for centuries, the statues which adorned the exterior of the Cathedral have always required maintenance: traces of early attempts at restoration have appeared during recent work by the Opificio delle Pietre Dure (literally, 'workshop of semi-precious stone' – the Florentine institute specialising in the restoration of sculpture). SIMONE DI FRANCESCO TALENTI's *Madonna* (below) was probably waterproofed with oils as protection against rain and damp, as appears from the stains visible on the surface of the marble: the oil has penetrated into the more porous areas. Lost or damaged parts have been replaced on the *Angel* by JACOPO DI PIERO GUIDI and on the *Virgin* attributed to a FOLLOWER OF GIOVANNI DI BALDUCCIO (right); the three elements forming the head and shoulders of the Virgin (which Annamaria Giusti has called "a sort of complicated assemblage") may be due to difficulties which arose during the process of manufacture.

sco Talenti; the two lateral aedicules contained the VIRGIN ANNUNCIATE and the ANGEL GABRIEL. The latter is probably by Jacopo di Piero Guidi and of the same date as Talenti's *Madonna*, whereas the *Virgin Annunciate*, attributed to a pupil of Giovanni di Balduccio, is half a century earlier; nevertheless, both these elegant sculptures clearly reveal the influence of northern Gothic.

On the right wall and beside the entrance there are six sculptures from the old façade of the Cathedral (→ pp. 24-25). Four of them represent musician angels and were located in the niches of the central doorway; the other two stood either side of the same doorway at the height of the second order.

From the left we have: ANGEL WITH REBECK (ca. 1388) by Luca di Giovanni da Siena; ST STEPHEN (ca. 1340-43) by Andrea Pisano; ANGEL WITH BAGPIPES (ca. 1388) by Luca di Giovanni da Siena; ANGEL WITH VIELLA (ca. 1385), PROPHET (ca. 1385) and ANGEL WITH CYMBALS (ca. 1383) by Jacopo di Piero Guidi.

Above, from the left: LUCA DI GIOVANNI DA SIENA, *Angel with a rebeck* (a three-stringed instrument that was played with a bow) and *Angel with bagpipes*; JACOPO DI PIERO GUIDI, *Angel with a viella* (an ancestor of the modern viola) and *Angel with cymbals*. Together with the *Angel with a lute* and the *Angel with an organ* by Piero di Giovanni Tedesco, displayed in the Room of the Old Façade (→ p. 40), these statues of musician angels probably adorned the central doorway of the façade designed by Arnolfo. After its demolition in 1587, they were all transferred to the Medici villa at Castello, with the single exception of the *Angel with a rebeck*, which was found in the garden of the Palazzo della Crocetta, now the Archaeological Museum. The Room of the Old Façade (right, seen from the first floor) was inaugurated in 1937. At the end of the room is the statue of Pope Boniface VIII, framed by Bandinelli's choir arch (→ pp. 56-57); the arch was transferred to the Museum when the choir was demolished in the 19th century.

From the passage we pass into the magnificent Room of the Old Façade.

5. The Room of the Old Façade

In this large rectangular room, which was inaugurated in 1937, is displayed the sculpture from the original façade of the Cathedral.

The façade designed by Arnolfo di Cambio was demolished in 1587 (→ pp. 24-25 and 162). To help us reconstruct its original appearance – apart from contemporary pictures that document the progress of work (the *Madonna of Mercy*, → p. 8, and the miniature of the *Miracle of St Zenobius*, → p. 24) – we have two valuable sources: a drawing "of almost photographic exactness" (Becherucci) made by BERNARDINO POCCETTI at the request of Bernardo Buontalenti (→ p. 25), and a detailed account of the demolition of the façade, compiled by an anonymous eyewitness. The drawing, which Poccetti reused for the background of his fresco in the first cloister of San Marco (*St Antoninus elected Archbishop of Florence*), was bequeathed to the Opera by Buontalenti (d. 1608); it is regarded as "the most reliable source in the entire literature on the cathedral façade" (Becherucci). The document was discovered in 1757 by Richa among the papers of Francesco Rondinelli. The words of the anonymous witness reveal his bitterness at the sight of so much wasteful destruction: "not a single marble was removed entire; the very columns were broken; it was truly a pitiable spectacle, principally in the ruination of the aforesaid façade, and secondly in the smashing of those marbles and porphyries so skillfully carved".

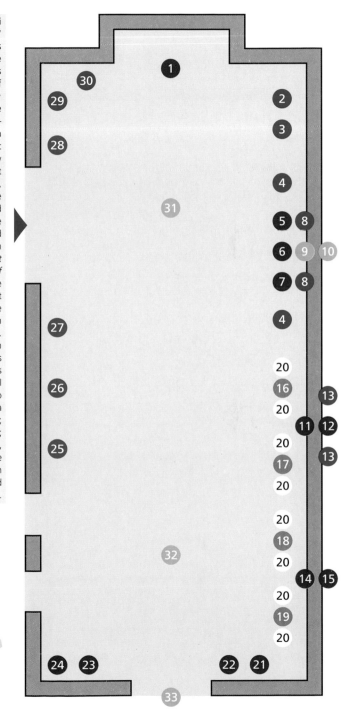

The first project for the façade was by Arnolfo di Cambio. By the time this great Tuscan architect came up with his design for the Cathedral, in the late 13th century, he had already had first-hand experience of two completely different cultures: in Rome he had studied and got to know the art of antiquity; in the kingdom of Naples – at that time still ruled by the Angevin dynasty from France – he became familiar with Northern-European gothic art.

The façade, of which Arnolfo (who died in the early years of the 14th century) managed to complete only the lower portion, took account of both influences, although its overall style is unmistakably classical. We can get a good idea of how it looked by examining the drawing made by Bernardino Poccetti in 1587, the year it was demolished. Certain features immediately attract our attention in this important document, the only record we possess of the original appearance of the façade (→ opposite). The characteristic vertical thrust of gothic architecture is here weakened by the horizontal divisions which impose a slow and measured rhythm. Even the elements derived from Northern-European architecture, such as the pointed arches above the lateral doors, and the niches containing statues, seem to be inserted into a context which considerably attenuates their impact. However accurate, Poccetti's drawing obviously conveys no idea of the brilliant colouring of the façade, with its white, green and pink marbles, and the golden mosaic decoration which Brunelleschi would have liked to extend to the interior of the dome (→ pp. 156-157).

After Arnolfo's death the façade remained unfinished because the architects who succeeded him – Giotto and Andrea Pisano – were chiefly occupied by the Campanile, whilst Francesco Talenti, who worked on the Cathedral between 1349 and 1359, enlarged the overall project but did not alter the outside. Until the mid-15th century, then, the sculptors who supplied statues for the façade worked from Arnolfo's design; towards the end of the century, however, completing the façade seemed less attractive than building a completely new one, and in 1490 a competition was announced. But Lorenzo the Magnificent, who was a member of the jury, wisely resolved to put off the decision until happier times; in this he demonstrated the good sense which was so obviously lacking in Grand Duke Francesco, when almost a century later (1587) he ordered the façade to be dismantled by Bernardo Buontalenti.

This architect – who nursed the ambition, frustrated by Francesco's death, of himself assuming the prestigious responsibility of building the new façade (→ p. 162-165) – took no trouble whatever to gather together or to safeguard the old sculptural decoration. Statues and reliefs thus suffered a process of dispersal – and sometimes of transformation or destruction – which makes it more difficult to identify the original locations of individual pieces.

Benedetto Caetani was born at Anagni in about 1235. In 1294 he was elected pope with the name of Boniface VIII after the *gran rifiuto* of Celestine V, whose abdication he seems to have encouraged. Celestine's death in the castle where the new pope had confined him unleashed a wave of accusations against Boniface, especially on the part of the Franciscan Spirituals. During his pontificate Boniface had to deal with two dreadful enemies: the French king Philip IV the Fair and the powerful Roman family of the Colonna. In order to raise money for the war against England, Philip decided to tax the clergy, an action forbidden by canon law. Boniface threatened him with excommunication (1296), but had to seek reconciliation after a violent insurrection by the Colonna, which he managed to quell only after a military campaign lasting a year. Peace with the king of France seemed to be sanctioned after the canonisation of Philip's grandfather Louis IX; but Philip continued to struggle against papal control of the clergy and had a French bishop imprisoned. Boniface demanded his release, but the States General closed ranks with the king. He therefore sought the assistance of Albert I of Habsburg, whom he appointed emperor in 1303. In a secret meeting at the Louvre Philip IV and his counsellor Guillaume de Nogaret launched a defamatory campaign against the pope (their accusations included heresy) and raised a demand for a General Council of the Church to depose him. Boniface was on the point of excommunicating Philip when on 7 September 1303 he was seized at Agnani by Nogaret and Sciarra Colonna with the connivance of certain cardinals and the complicity of local nobles who, however, soon repented, and released him after a couple of days. Probably roughly manhandled and certainly destroyed in spirit, Boniface died shortly after his return to Rome.

The statue of Boniface VIII

Immediately to our left, framed by a large marble arch from the 16th-century choir of the Cathedral (→ p. 56-57), we find the monument to POPE BONIFACE VIII, made in 1 the final years of the 13th century by Arnolfo di Cambio and his assistants. Originally flanked by statues of a deacon and an assistant, now headless in a private Florentine garden, this portrait of the pope was undoubtedly at one time on the façade, although it is not shown in the drawing by Poccetti (→ p. 25).

After the dismantling of the façade in the 16th century this statue suffered much ill-treatment, the most serious being the incompetent restoration carried out between the 17th and 18th century, which partly ruined its appearance: the front portion of the drapery was reworked, and the sides, where the pope's vestments formed a series of folds, were smoothed off. In 1893 we find it in the possession of the antiques dealer Stefano Bardini, founder of the Bardini Museum; from him it was acquired by Onorato Caetani di Sermoneta, a distant descendant of Boniface's, who presented it to the Cathedral. It stood on the counter-façade until 1937, when it was moved into the Museum together with the 19th-century stone base bearing an Italian inscription ("This portrait of Boniface VIII, from the original but now dismantled façade of our Cathedral, recorded for three centuries its foundation, while he was pope, in 1296, and after three more centuries was munificently recovered and returned to the sacred site by the generosity and civic piety of Onorato Caetani, Duke of Sermoneta, as the venerable relic of memories eternalised in history").

Despite the restorations we have mentioned, the statue has managed to preserve intact its aura of holiness and of classical composure. The fact that it stood on the façade of the Cathedral had a precise political significance: Boniface VIII, who ruled the Church during one of the most turbulent periods in the Middle Ages, protected and defended the Guelf communes against the Empire, causing him to be honoured by various monuments while still alive (apart from this one in Florence, there were others in Rome, Orvieto, Anagni and Bologna).

The other statues from the façade

Along the wall opposite the entrance, from the left, we find two statues of PROPHETS (ca. 1310). At one time standing on the central buttresses of the façade or on those of 2-3

A stern and impulsive man, hated as the champion of the Church's primacy over the nascent national monarchies, Pope Boniface VIII is remembered in particular for the famous Bull *Unam Sanctam* (1302), affirming the supremacy of the spiritual over the temporal power. Also well know are the sarcastic phrases spoken of him by Dante in the *Divine Comedy*: "servant of the servants", "the great priest – may ill befall him!", "the prince of the new Pharisees". The poet, indeed, condemns Boniface to the bolgia of the simoniacs. Dante's bitterness is to be explained by the political situation in Florence, which by the late 13th century was split into the two warring factions of Blacks (or traditional Guelfs) and the Whites (who were of Ghibelline tendency). Having made various unsuccessful attempts at reconciliation, Boniface summoned Charles de Valois, brother of King Philip the Fair, and conferred on him full powers to pacify the city: after five months of partisan administration the Whites (including Dante) were all exiled or ruined. The many statues erected to honour Boniface – turned by the Colonna into an accusation of idolatry – confirm the fact that he raised the height of the papal tiara and added to it at least one crown, and possibly two. On the occasion of the great Jubilee he indicted for the year 1300 (the first Holy Year known to us) he restored and embellished many Roman churches. For the construction of Florence's new cathedral he set aside a "bond of three thousand golden florins" (10 February 1296). He rearranged and augmented the Vatican Library (dispersed in 1227), which after his death could boast the largest collection of Greek manuscripts in the West. Celebrated miniaturists such as Oderisi da Gubbio and Franco Bolognese worked for him. He himself produced the *Liber sextus* of the Pontifical Constitutions. In 1303 he founded in Rome the University 'La Sapienza'.

The two architectural fragments above the *Madonna of the Glass Eyes* (the lunette from the central doorway and a piece of architrave, → p. 42) help us to reconstruct, even if only partially, the original appearance of Arnolfo's façade. The overall effect must have been spectacular: the rich sculptural decoration was displayed against a precious background of marbles (white from Carrara, red from Siena, green serpentine from Prato) and mosaics made by the Cosmati masters whom Arnolfo had worked with in Rome. In his plans for the Cathedral, which Becherucci has called "the first renaissance edifice in Florence", the architect makes use of that synthesis of the ancient and the modern which is the keynote of his art. The elements proper to late Gothic (e.g. the taste in decoration) are accompanied in Arnolfo by the rediscovery – which is also a re-evaluation – of the architectural tradition of the past, from the antique to early-Christian and Romanesque. The rounded sense of unity and balance we find in his works derives from this "reaffirmation in modern terms of an uninterrupted tradition": an approach to the antique which links this 'borderland' artist to the sensibility of the Renaissance. The son of Cambio and of Madonna Perfetta, Arnolfo was born in Colle Valdelsa around 1245. The pupil and collaborator of Nicola Pisano, he followed him to Bologna and Siena. He worked in Rome, Viterbo, Perugia and Orvieto, making funerary monuments for cardinals and popes (→ p. 16). In Florence, in addition to his great works on the Cathedral, he directed various building-sites which were radically to transform the outlook of the city: Palazzo Vecchio, the church of Santa Croce, the Badia Fiorentina. The city did not remain indifferent: by a Priors' decree (1 April 1300) he was exonerated from paying taxes of any kind for the whole of his natural life (*donec vixerit*).

the left doorway, they are now in poor condition, especially the first which is headless. Both of them are from the workshop of Arnolfo di Cambio and were discovered in the early 20th century in a garden in Via della Scala, at one time part of the extensive Orti Oricellari. The head of the complete statue seems to have been inspired by one of the Dacian prisoners on Trajan's Column; we may assume that the head of the other Prophet was also derived from the antique.

The decorative scheme of Arnolfo's façade was devoted to the Virgin, as indeed was the whole Cathedral. In particular, the lunette above the left doorway showed the *Madonna of the Nativity*; the central doorway had the *Virgin enthroned between St Reparata and St Zenobius and Angels*; above the right door was the *Dormitio Virginis* or Death of the Virgin. To the right of the two *Prophets* we come to the Virgin enthroned from the main doorway, 6 flanked by St Reparata holding an oil-lamp as a symbol of her virginity, and by St Zenobius in episcopal vestments. The hieratic pose of the Virgin, sculpted by Arnolfo in the early years of the 14th century, still reflects the Byzantine tradition; what is quite new is its sense of solid, realistic physicality which relates it to the painting of Giotto. Arnolfo's realism extends to the pupils of the Virgin's eyes, which are made of vitreous paste, so the statue came to be known as the Madonna of the Glass Eyes. Immediately after the dismantling of the façade this statue was moved inside the Cathedral, where it became the focus of popular

Above, a *Prophet* attributed to the WORKSHOP OF ARNOLFO DI CAMBIO. Below, right, the *Madonna of the Glass Eyes* (centre) and *St Reparata* (left) by ARNOLFO DI CAMBIO, and *St Zenobius* (right), by his workshop. The anonymous eye-witness (→ p. 23) writes that above the main (i.e. central) doorway of the Cathedral "there stood a fair and beautiful aedicule, in which was a marble image of Our Lady seated with the Child, who with most beautiful grace was sitting on her knee, and she had shining eyes which seemed real as they were made of glass" (the only instance in Florentine sculpture). The Operai took a different view; they judged the statue "monstrous and ridiculous, as it has eyes of glass, and hideous proportions". In its "archaic, almost idol-like majesty" the *Madonna* shows the influence of ancient models; but the sense of volume, the rhythm of chiaroscuro effects, and the rigorous geometrical composition reveal the hand of an innovator.

devotion. There was talk of miracles, and the ecclesiastical authorities, with the prudence typical of the Counter-Reformation period, decided to remove the statue in case its presence should give rise to superstition. So it was that the Virgin (although there had been plans to make a special tabernacle for it in the Piazza del Grano) found its way to the Opera.

Also by Arnolfo di Cambio is the ST REPARATA to the left 5 of the *Madonna*. This sculpture, close to the Virgin both in date and style, was rediscovered in 1917 in a niche of the amphitheatre in the Boboli Gardens, where it had been mistaken for a Roman statue. The ST ZENOBIUS, of 7 more modest workmanship, is a piece of the same date from Arnolfo's workshop.

The whole complex is surmounted by two CURTAIN-HOLD- 8 ING ANGELS from the workshop of Arnolfo, which completed the sculptural decoration on the central doorway, and is flanked by two series of eight statuettes arranged in two rows. They are the SAINTS which stood in the small 4 niches decorating the splays of the central doorway. Made

The destruction of Arnolfo's original façade was an irreparable disaster for Italian art, which lost one of its masterpieces, and also for scholars, who lost the principal point of departure for a reconstruction of the artistic history of the period. It is not surprising that in some cases critics have been seriously misled: a mistaken interpretation of some archive documents and of several fragments discovered on the old façade by the architect Emilio De Fabris, for example, gave rise to the theory that Arnolfo's façade had been bare of sculpture. On these pages, two views of the wall facing the entrance: opposite, the left half with the *Madonna of the Glass Eyes* (beneath, the *Saint* attributed to Francesco del Sellaio); below, the right half with the *Madonna of the Nativity* and the cast of the *Dormitio Virginis*, all by Arnolfo.

between 1387 and 1390, these little sculptures are almost all by an artist probably from Milan, Piero di Giovanni Tedesco, who worked on the Cathedral for almost twenty years and introduced into Florence several decorative motifs from northern Gothic: the only exception is the second statuette in the lower row on the left, which is attributed to Francesco del Sellaio and dated ca. 1350-1375.

Moving to the right, we see high on the wall the sculpture from the lunette over the left doorway. This MADONNA OF THE NATIVITY by Arnolfo, with its face touched by melancholy, is marked by a classicism which relates it closely to the portrait of Boniface VIII. The two ANGELS from the spandrels of the lunette are from Arnolfo's workshop; immediately above the Madonna is a fragment of the ANNOUNCEMENT TO THE SHEPHERDS (ca. 1310), which came from the aedicule to the right of the lunette.

Next, also high up, there is a cast of the DORMITIO VIRGINIS (or *Death of the Virgin*), at one time on the lunette over the right doorway. Arnolfo's original, badly damaged by aerial bombardment in the second world war, is now in

Right, the *Madonna of the Nativity* by Arnolfo di Cambio. The diligent eye-witness wrote: "above the door which is beside the main one on the left-hand side, towards the Via Martelli, inside another aedicule was sculpted the Nativity of Our Lord [the *Madonna of the Nativity*] with many figures of Shepherds and Animals. Above the other door, which is towards the Campanile, there was represented the Passing of Mary [the *Dormitio Virginis*] with many statues, in which we saw her lying dead, and Christ holding her Soul tightly in his arms, and all the Apostles, who surrounded the dead body". The *Madonna of the Nativity* was discovered in 1904 by Swarzenski in the *bottega* of the antiques dealer Bardini, together with other sculptures (including the *Dormitio Virginis*, which was then acquired by the Berlin Museum. Identification was made possible not only by the passage we have just quoted but also by the drawing by Poccetti (→ pp. 23 25), where however the *Dormitio* is replaced by a *Deposition*. Luisa Becherucci provides a careful stylistic analysis: "beginning the decoration of the Florentine façade with the *Boniface VIII* and with the *Nativity*, the first chapter of his Marian cycle, [Arnolfo] had not yet turned from that subtly intellectual classicism which had marked his later Roman works". She considers that in this work the sculptor had not yet attained that "grandiose expressive concentration" which we find in the *Dormitio*, in the *St Reparata* and in the *Madonna and Child*. Below, the *St Victor* attributed to Nanni di Banco, flanked by a pair of *Adoring Angels*. St Victor and St Barnabas were venerated on account of the victories won by Florence over the Pisans at Cascina and over the Aretines at Certomondo, on their respective feast-days. Opposite, the *Doctors of the Church* by Niccolò Lamberti (the two to the left of the door) and by Piero di Giovanni Tedesco (the two to the right).

the Bode-Museum in Berlin, having been acquired on the antiques market. According to an old document, next to the dead body of the Virgin stood the figure of Christ, holding in his arms the soul of his Mother; all that now remains of this scene are the two HEADS placed above the Virgin. The group was originally surrounded by the twelve Apostles.   15

Lower down on the wall are the four statues of saints which formerly flanked the central doorway at the height of the second order. These works, each of which is flanked by a pair of Adoring Angels, date from the late 14th century, when work on the façade was momentarily resumed. From left to right we find the cast of St Stephen, St Victor (head-   20

16-1[

less, with a cloak), the cast of ST LAURENCE, and ST BARNABAS (also headless). The originals of the two casts, now in the Louvre in Paris, are by Piero di Giovanni Tedesco; so too, it would seem, is the ST BARNABAS, while the ST VICTOR is to be regarded as a youthful work by Nanni di Banco.

Turning now to the short right-hand wall, we find four late-14th-century statues of the four Doctors of the Church. To the left of the door leading to the Room of the Paintings we find ST AUGUSTINE and ST GREGORY THE GREAT by Niccolò 21-24 di Piero Lamberti; to the right of the door, ST AMBROSE and ST JEROME by Piero di Giovanni Tedesco. These sculptures, very much wasted, stood originally in the upper niches of the buttresses on the façade; after the 1587 dismantling, they metamorphosed into laurel-crowned portraits of Homer, Virgil, Dante and Petrarch, and until 1936 decorated the entrance to the Viale del Poggio Imperiale.

Opposite, Nanni di Banco, *St Luke*. This statue – for which Nanni received payments in 1410, 1412 and 1413 (the final payment) – occupied the second of the two niches to the left of the central door. Before the *Isaias* (1408) was attributed to him, the *St Luke* was the first and only dated work by the artist. Born around 1390, Nanni di Antonio di Banco matriculated in 1405 in the guild of stonecutters and woodworkers. Between 1407 and 1408 he was engaged on the Porta della Mandorla, and then on Orsanmichele. Characterised by a serene classical style, he was wrongly thought by Vasari to have been a pupil of Donatello, who was in fact his contemporary and friend. For further information on Nanni, see the recent study by Mary Bergstein, who in addition to his certain works examines many doubtfully-attributed sculptures displayed in this Museum.

We turn now to the second long wall. Poccetti's drawing of the façade allows us to locate exactly the statues of the four EVANGELISTS, which filled the four large niches flanking the central doorway: ST LUKE by Nanni di Banco, ST JOHN by Donatello, ST MATTHEW by Bernardo Ciuffagni and ST MARK (beyond the entrance to the passage) by Niccolò di Piero Lamberti.   25-28

The statues were made between 1408 and 1415; after the destruction of the façade in 1587 they were placed inside the Cathedral, where they remained until 1936. Although of unequal artistic value, these four works effectively illustrate the chief tendencies of Florentine sculpture of that time.

The ST MARK appears typically gothic, especially in the treatment of the beard and the drapery, which lends the figure a wholly external pathos.   28

Very different is the impression of proud serenity conveyed by the ST LUKE, shown reading a sacred book. The forms of the body emerge clearly from beneath the sober drapery, and the down-turned gaze heightens the figure's sense of concentrated vitality.   25

Right and opposite, the *St John the Evangelist* by Donatello. The statue was commissioned from the artist by the Opera del Duomo in 1408 and was carved in the Cathedral, in a chapel at the side of the tribune of St Zenobius, which in July 1410 was closed off to protect the work in progress from prying eyes. The sculptor took his time. A resolution issued in April 1415 and notified to Donatello by the Opera's messenger Fermalpunto, demanded that he finish the *St John* by the following May, or be fined 25 florins; in October the statue was finished, it was assessed at 160 florins, and paid for. Donato di Niccolò di Betto Bardi, better known as Donatello, was probably the greatest Italian sculptor of the Renaissance; it would be reductive merely to see in him, as has sometimes been done, the first sparks of the genius of Michelangelo (whose celebrated *Moses* is held to derive from this *St John*). "Delighting in everything, he set his hand to all things" (Vasari); a curious and experimental artist, the author of what is regarded as the first renaissance sculpture (the *St George* of Orsanmichele), he studied and understood the art of antiquity better than anyone else, but always sought to explore new territories, in the company of the great intellectuals of his time, though he was not himself one of them. Giorgio Vasari, writing in 1550, could still say of Donatello that "in our age none has equalled him". The Museum's collection allows the visitor to follow almost every stage in the creative journey of this exceptional artist, who was born in Florence around 1386 and began his career as an assistant to Lorenzo Ghiberti: his participation in the decoration of the façade and his much-debated work on the Porta della Mandorla (→ pp. 66-70), the many statues of *Prophets* for the Campanile, the Cantoria for the Canons' Sacristy (→ pp. 100-115) and the wooden statue of the *Magdalene* (→ pp. 118-119).

Below, the *St Mark* by Niccolò di Piero Lamberti. Between the corbels decorating its base is the inscription *OPUS NICHOLAI*; the presence of the sculptor's signature has not prevented scholars from discussing the attribution for centuries. The marble blocks for the *Evangelists* were ready in 1405, when Lorenzo di Giovanni d'Ambrogio and Niccolò Lamberti were sent to Carrara to rough-hew them; they lay in Pisa during the war with Milan, and did not arrive in Florence until 1407. In December 1408 three of them were entrusted to Niccolò Lamberti, Donatello and Nanni di Banco on the understanding that the fourth block (and the fourth *Evangelist*) would be assigned to the one who had best worked his own. Time, however, was running out, and in 1410 the *St Matthew* (opposite) was commissioned from Bernardo Ciuffagni. The undeniable imitation of Donatello's *St John* which one notices in this work perhaps explains the Operai's decision to close off the chapels where the statues were being carved, "so that they cannot be seen". Right, the *Angel with a lute* and the *Angel with an organ* by Piero di Giovanni Tedesco.

Donatello's St John strikes us with its powerful chiaroscuro effects in the lower portion, achieved by the deep cutting of the drapery. The Saint is shown in an exhausted attitude, emphasised by the limp and inert arms. The intensity of his gaze turned to our left, the bushy brows slightly frowning, and the horizontal crease across his forehead suggest prophetic vision, as though Donatello had sought to portray not so much the Evangelist as the seer of the *Apocalypse*. 26

In the St Matthew Bernardo Ciuffagni demonstrates what he has learned from Lorenzo Ghiberti about the treatment of drapery. The pose of the figure, on the other hand, is too close to that of the *St John* for us to think it accidental. We know that Donatello sculpted his Evangelist inside the Cathedral, shrouding his work in the greatest possible secrecy; Ciuffagni, however, must have sneaked a glimpse of the model, if not of the actual statue while it was being carved. 27

To the right of the *St Mark* by Niccolò di Pietro Lamberti and on the short wall to the left of the *Boniface VIII*, there are two more MUSICIAN ANGELS (one with a lute, the other with an organ) by Piero di Giovanni Tedesco, which were also intended for the splays of the central doorway (→ pp. 21-22). 29-30

Sun worship is a feature common to many ancient civilisations, although only rarely did it develop into a true solar religion. In Indo-European cultures (Indo-Iranian, Graeco-Roman and Scandinavian) the sun-god drives his chariot across the sky; he is, however, a minor deity compared with the powerful sky-god (Zeus, Jupiter); Helios, for example, became progressively identified with Apollo. Solar cults achieved renewed importance in late antiquity: the feast of the Unconquered Sun on 25 December was eventually assimilated to Christmas, celebrating the nativity of Christ. The *Dioskouroi* ('sons of Zeus') were also popular divinities in the ancient world, invoked by armies and sailors in difficulty. According to myth, Castor was the son of Leda and of Tindarus, king of Sparta, while Pollux (together with Helen, whose rape caused the Trojan War) was born from the union of Leda with Zeus, who coupled with her in the form of a swan. So as not to be separated from Castor, Pollux renounced his immortality; transformed by Zeus into the constellation Gemini, the brothers divide their time between the heavens and the underworld.

The other pieces

Near the statue of Boniface VIII, resting on three corbels with lion's heads, is a ROMAN SARCOPHAGUS of the 2nd century AD, another curious example of the medieval habit of recycling antique marbles. In 1363 Piero da Farnese, the commander of the Florentine militia, died of the Plague. A few months earlier he had defeated the Pisans in the fierce engagement of Bagno a Vena, showing such heroism that the Republic decided to honour his memory by erecting, four years later, a funerary monument in the Cathedral. The antique sarcophagus was reworked on three sides, so that the original sculpture remained only on the side facing the wall. On the lid stood a statue of the commander, probably in wood and plaster, which was lost when the tomb was dismantled in the 19th century.

The surviving original side of the sarcophagus shows three scenes from one of the many versions of the Greek myth of Phaethon ('Shining'). In the first scene, the young man appears with his father Helios (the Sun) and his sisters, the Heliades. In the centre, Phaethon has taken control of the chariot which Helios uses to drive through the sky, giving light to the world; but in his unpractised hands the horses lurch off course, threatening to burn the whole world, so Zeus strikes him down with a thunderbolt, and his body falls into the river Eridanus. To the right, Castor and Pollux retrieve the horses and lead them back to Olympus; behind them appear Hesperos and Eosphoros, that is to say Phaethon himself under the form of the star

31

Opposite: the Roman side of the Farnese sarcophagus dates from the 2nd century AD and illustrates the myth of Phaethon. Above, the medieval side of the sarcophagus, once coloured (there are traces of gilding, of blue and of red); right, the two ends. It now seems certain that the equestrian statue which surmounted the sarcophagus, and was attributed to Andrea Orcagna or to his brother Jacopo, has been lost for good; its disappearance is somewhat mysterious, however, because well into the 19th century it is said to have lain in the deposits of the Opera. Authorities differ as to its materials: wood and papier-mâché, wood and canvas, plaster and papier-mâché. It is certain, however, that Piero was portrayed riding a rearing mule – a posture to be widely used in centuries to come. The statue was inspired by an incident that occurred during the battle of Bagno a Vena: his horse slain from under him, Farnese did not lose heart, but fought on to victory mounted on a pack-mule.

he personifies: Aphrodite, the Roman Venus. It is a double form because Venus is at the same time both the brightest star in the evening (Hesperos, the Latin *Vesper*) and the bringer of morning (Eosphoros – *Lucifer* to the Latins – means 'bearer of the dawn' in Greek).

The other long side of the sarcophagus has, alternating with fields semé-de-lis, three coats of arms: the lily of Florence, the Guelf eagle, and the cross of the People. The right short side has the Farnese arms surmounted by a helm with crest; on the left side, from the bottom, there is another Farnese coat of arms, a helm, an upside-down fox – the symbol of the defeated Pisans – and a small Far-

nese lily. The cover, placed in front of the sarcophagus, is decorated with lilies on an azure ground, and bears the papal symbol of the Keys of St Peter.

The second piece, opposite the door of the Room of the Paintings, is a HOLY-WATER STOUP (ca. 1380) by Jacopo di 32 Piero Guidi. The ANGEL WITH BASIN on top of it is by an anonymous 15th-century artist and replaced an earlier one, as appears from a lunette frescoed by Fabrizio Boschi in the first cloister of San Marco, showing *St Antoninus driving the curious out of the Duomo* (early 17th century). In the Cathedral the stoup was replaced, probably in the 19th century, by a copy.

The architectural fragments

Our tour of this room concludes with three interesting architectural fragments. The first is the pointed LUNETTE in 9 pink marble and mosaic, behind the 'Madonna of the Glass Eyes'. We can get a good idea of the bright colouring of the original façade not only from this lunette, whose present position corresponds to its original one, but also from the architectural element we see above. It is a PIECE OF 10 ARCHITRAVE or the lower cornice of a window, a large fragment in marble and gilded and coloured mosaic, decorated with five rectangular coffers and surrounded on three sides by a frieze.

Finally, high up on the short right-hand wall there is the TRACERY from a 14th-century three-lighted window from 33 the Campanile.

We now go up three steps and enter the renewed Room of the Paintings.

The *Angel with a vase* (above) which surmounted the holy-water stoup of JACOPO DI PIERO GUIDI has been attributed to URBANO DI PIETRO DA CORTONA. Right, the tracery of a window from the Campanile.

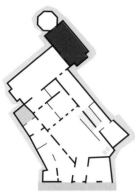

6. The Room of the Paintings

In the 14th century the Cathedral was crammed with altars, chapels and funerary monuments. The altars, mostly of wood, were to be found along the aisles, against the counter-façade and even against the large piers. This typically medieval arrangement was completely altered after Brunelleschi had built the dome and the chapels of the apse: the new sense of unified internal space was incompatible with the presence of so many structures blocking the view of the whole and upsetting the harmonious uniformity of the in-

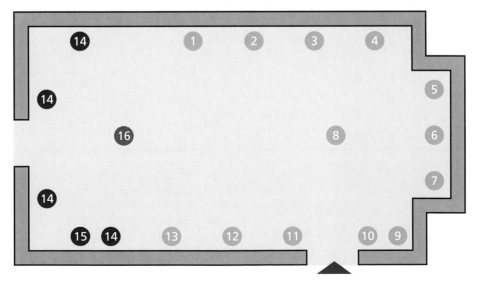

In many of the paintings displayed in this room we find the patron saints of Florence, protectors of the city walls and of the inhabitants, to whom they guaranteed peace, health and prosperity; this is hardly surprising, as the works come from the Cathedral, the religious heart of Florence. The principal patron is naturally St John the Baptist, the Precursor, to whom the oldest and best loved of the city's churches was dedicated: the Baptistery. St John is often accompanied by the other two traditional patrons: St Zenobius, bishop of Florence in the 4th century (→ p. 45; below, in a wood inlay by GIULIANO DA MAIANO in the Sacristy of the Masses), and St Reparata, the martyr to whom the cathedral had been dedicated (→ p. 46). Veneration for saints such as Victor and Barnabas was connected to victories obtained by Florence on their feast days, taken as a sign of their favour for the city.

terior. Behind this intolerance one can detect the first signs of the 'cultural revolution' of the Renaissance, determined by the canons of regularity and symmetry, a revolution which did not spare the many altarpieces and smaller painted panels at that time on the altars. This was the beginning of a process of dispersal of the Cathedral's paintings, which was to increase over the centuries and to spare only those works that were the objects of intense devotion. The final and decisive intervention was that of the architect Gaetano Baccani, who in 1838 removed the remaining altars from the side walls and the counter-façade: the paintings which decorated them were removed to the deposits of the Opera and thence to the Museum. A different fate unfortunately met many of the panels removed in earlier centuries, and the documentation on the original pictorial patrimony of the Cathedral is by no means complete. The surviving works, gathered into this room of the Museum, were mostly in poor condition: a campaign of restoration carried out over a number of years has fortunately brought about the gradual recovery of this collection, so full of art-historical and documentary interest.

The paintings

On the main wall opposite the entrance, starting from the left, we come first to the celebrated tempera panel depicting ST ZENOBIUS BETWEEN ST EUGENIUS AND ST CRESCENTIUS, 1 WITH SCENES FROM HIS LIFE. This altar dossal, of great artistic value and of devotional importance, dates from the mid-13th century and is attributed to the Master of the Bigallo. We notice two fundamental characteristics: stylistic elegance typical of the Byzantine manner, and a sense of form and of narrative tension which, several decades before Giotto, already distinguish Florentine painting. In evaluating this masterpiece we must unfortunately make allowance for heavy repainting carried out over the centuries: a restoration in 1937 eliminated most of it but did not succeed in recovering the original face of the Saint, which we now see in a 15th-century reworking; furthermore, the scenes in the upper register have two large lacunae caused by detachment of the painted surface.

In the centre of the rectangular panel we see St Zenobius seated on a throne, dressed in bishop's vestments, with mitre and crosier; at his sides, in dalmatics, are St Eugenius (left, with book) and St Crescentius (right, with book and thurible). At the sides, four rectangular scenes show miracles worked by Zenobius during his life. Between Zenobius

Above, the *dossal of St Zenobius*, attributed to the author of the *Crucifix* now in the Bigallo Museum (and known as the Master of the Bigallo). Zenobius was born around 340, in a Florence that was still mainly pagan, to the noble family of the Girolami, who owned a tower in Por Santa Maria. He succeeded Theodore as bishop of Florence and encountered Ambrose when the latter came to consecrate the basilica of San Lorenzo. The miracles attributed to Zenobius have been illustrated by Florentine artists for centuries. Especially famous was the miracle of the elm, which according to legend took place during the transferral of the saint's mortal remains from his bishop's seat of San Lorenzo to the new cathedral of Santa Reparata: the event – right, in a miniature by COSIMO ROSSELLI (*Edili* 148, fol. 58v) – is recorded by the Column of St Zenobius, on the north side of the Baptistery. We now know that this transferral took place not, as one might suppose from the date given on the dossal, immediately after the saint's death, but many years later, at the end of the 9th century. On the occasion of the Council of Florence (1439) the body of the bishop was once again transferred, this time to the crypt beneath the chancel of the Cathedral. In 1685 his remains were placed inside the bronze ark made by Ghiberti.

and Eugenius, low down, an inscription in several lines reads: QUESTA·TA / VOLA·FU·FATA / DE·L·OLMO·DE / LA·PI-AZA / GENAIO CCCCXXV / IIII ("This panel was made from the elm in the piazza, January 429"). According to the legend, the solemn translation of the Saint's mortal remains from the basilica of San Lorenzo to the cathedral of Santa Reparata was accompanied by a miracle: on the north side of the Baptistery there grew an old elm tree, and as the bier with the Saint's body passed beneath it a branch, withered by the winter cold, burst suddenly into leaf. We can easily imagine the devotional importance of a picture painted on the actual wood taken from this miraculous tree.

The panel depicting *St Reparata between St John the Baptist and St Zenobius* (right) is attributed to Lorenzo di Niccolò (early 15th century). Concerning the life of this Saint there are two traditions: the first, which traces her origin to Caesarea, makes her a victim of the persecution of Decius; according to the second, she was a young maiden who entered a monastery disguised in male attire, and was put to death for having seduced a nun: when the mistake was discovered she was buried with full honours, and penances were performed in reparation (whence the name 'Reparata'). In Florence the cult of St Reparata was linked to the victory gained on 8 October (her feast day) 405 over the army of Radagaisus, "king of the Goths and Vandals", who besieged the city with "two hundred thousand horsemen"; it seems that the Saint herself appeared in the sky with the banner of the Cross to protect the walls of Florence. A tradition recorded by the chronicler Matteo Villani connects this incident with the dedication of the old cathedral. The panel was placed above the sarcophagus of St Zenobius in the cathedral crypt. Here, as elsewhere, Reparata is portrayed together with the other two city's patron saints. Below, the beheading of the Saint.

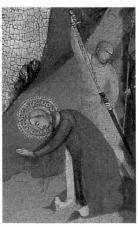

The next panel was until recently in very poor condition, also on account of repainting; careful restoration has recovered the original brilliant colours and has removed later additions. The picture dates from the early 15th century and represents St Reparata. The martyr is holding the standard with the cross of the Florentine People (gules on a ground argent), the palm of martyrdom, and a book. Beside the figure are four scenes of her martyrdom: in the first (top left), the emperor Decius (248-251) has molten lead poured over her; in the second (top right), red-hot irons, held by pincers are applied to her breasts; in the third (centre left), she is thrown into a blazing furnace; in the fourth (centre right), she is beheaded, and blood streams from her severed neck (the restorer has eliminated the later addition of a white dove, representing Repara-

Below, the panel depicting *St John the Baptist between St Zenobius and St Reparata* by the MASTER OF THE MEDICI POLYPTYCH (earlier 14th-century). This work shows the influence of Pacino di Buonaguida and Bernardo Daddi. The polyptych from which its anonymous author takes his name is in the church of Santa Croce, divided between the high altar and the Medici Chapel.

ta's soul leaving her body). In the lower register there is St John the Baptist on the left, and St Zenobius on the right.

The original location of the third painting on this wall is unknown. It is a triptych showing ST JOHN THE BAPTIST BE- 3 TWEEN ST ZENOBIUS AND ST REPARATA, dating from the earlier 14th century and attributed to the anonymous Master of the Polyptych of the Medici Chapel. Two coats of arms of the commissioning family, painted at the base of the shutters, were erased centuries ago, and their illegibility

contributes to the mystery which still surrounds the triptych's provenance.

After a very fine St Catherine of Alexandria attributed   4
to Bernardo Daddi, we come to the first short wall.

The first painting on the left is a pointed panel with a
background of gold leaf, showing the Judgement of St Ivo.   5
The patron saint of lawyers and notaries is shown seated
and wrapped in a red cloak. At lower left a woman proffers a parchment, probably a contract; on the right a male
figure, possibly a merchant, holds a purse full of money.
The shape and background of the panel are somewhat in-

Above, Bernardo Daddi, *St Catherine
of Alexandria*. The beautiful maiden
who confounded fifty philosophers
and won the heart of the emperor
Maxentius (who even offered her
the crown) was extremely popular.
We see her here with her traditional
attributes: the palm of martyrdom
in one hand, a book in the other,
and the nailed wheel (the rejected
emperor sent her to be tortured,
but the nails on the wheel broke);
we shall find the book and the
wheel of the philosopher saint also
in the painting by Giovanni del
Biondo (→ pp. 54-55) and in the
chapel altarpiece (→ p. 61). As
always, Daddi's line is of supreme
elegance: a follower of Giotto, he
devised a soft, fluid style which
had great success and showed the
influence both of the Sienese and
of Maso di Banco (Longhi). Right,
the *Judgement of St Ivo*. This
Breton saint, who used a textbook
of jurisprudence as a pillow and
was known as 'the advocate of the
poor', lived in the 13th century.

congruous in view of the period in which it was painted,
the later 15th century. The artist is unknown, although
the name of Neri di Bicci has been suggested. The original location is unknown.

Next comes the TRIPTYCH OF ST SEBASTIAN (ca. 1375-1380), 6
attributed to Giovanni del Biondo. The central panel
shows the martyrdom of the Saint, lashed to a stake and
pierced by an enormous number of arrows; from the right
an angel brings the crown of martyrdom; at the bottom are
the archers, and at the far right a man crowned with laurel, perhaps the emperor, and a bearded pagan priest. On
the left panel the Saint is shown preaching (above), and in-
terceding during the Plague (below); on the right the
Saint, beaten to death and flung into the Cloaca Maxima
(above), appears to Lucilla to show her where his body is
buried (below). In the left cusp there is the Archangel
Gabriel, in the right cusp the Virgin Annunciate, and in
the central pointed cusp Christ in benediction with the
open book bearing the letters Alpha and Omega, symbol

of eternity. The proposed dating of this triptych is based on the Saint represented: Sebastian, who was invoked for protection against the bubonic plague. In 1374, just a quarter of a century after the terrible 'Black Death' of 1348, Florence was afflicted by a new and less severe outbreak of the disease: it is likely that this painting was a splendid ex-voto offered in thanksgiving by a survivor. We might add that the symbolic connection between arrows – which Sebastian survived – and epidemics derives from antiquity: the *Iliad*, for instance, begins with the plague caused by the invisible shafts fired at the Greek army by Apollo and his divine sister Artemis.

The next panel comes from the Cathedral. It is a tempera of the Florentine school showing the MADONNA SUCKLING THE CHILD BETWEEN ST JOHN THE BAPTIST AND ST BLAISE (earlier 14th century). This sacred image has been known by various names: in the 15th century it was generally called the *Madonna of the Stoup*, because it was on an altar near to the holy-water vessel, but the faithful also referred to it as the *Madonna of the Snow* and the *Madonna of the Arrow*, on account of two miracles connected with it. The concourse of people thronging about it was so great that in 1646 it had to be moved to a less central position, on an altar in one of the chapels in the left tribune: around 1840 it was finally removed and placed in the rooms of the Opera.

A transparent case in the centre of the room contains the PROCESSIONAL PANEL OF ST AGATHA, showing an image of the Saint on each side. The earlier one (facing the wall opposite the entrance) dates from the mid-13th century and is

Opposite, *Madonna enthroned suckling the Child between St John the Baptist and St Blaise* (earlier 14th century). Above, the *processional panel of St Agatha* seen from the older, 13th-century side, framed in carved and gilded wood; this very frame is mentioned in some documentary notes of the early 16th century recording payments made to "Antonio the woodworker for having made an ornament for a wooden panel of St Agatha to be carried in procession". The learned 18th-century scholar Giuseppe Richa – whose ten-volume work *Notizie istoriche delle chiese fiorentine, divise ne' suoi quartieri* (1754-1762) is a mine of valuable information – says he discovered in "an old book in the sacristy of Santa Reparata containing the feasts and functions of the church" that the image was carried in procession by the entire clergy "on the fifth day of February, the feast of St Agatha, since this Saint is an advocate against fire". Right, MASTER OF ST AGATHA (mid-13th century) and JACOPO LANDINI known as JACOPO DEL CASENTINO (earlier 14th century), *St Agatha*.

Right, mosaic of the *Creation of Eve* (vault of the Baptistery, north segment, third register) attributed to COPPO DI MARCOVALDO, perhaps the author of the older side of the processional panel of St Agatha. Influenced in his early career by Giunta Pisano, Coppo (ca. 1225-1280) was, together with Meliore, the dominant figure in Florentine painting before Cimabue. In the Baptistery of San Giovanni, his workshop was responsible for the *Hell* and for the telamons of the apse, while the *Last Judgement* was made in collaboration with the workshop of Meliore. Coppo's style in characterised by a sense of power and passion unknown to the "frozen solemnity" (Gombrich) of the Byzantine tradition; the irregular, repetitive and obsessive rhythm of some of his works has its parallel in the poetry of Jacopone da Todi. Opposite, the quatrefoils of LORENZO DI BICCI (left) and MARIOTTO DI NARDO (right). Until Baccani's purist restoration they were part of the decoration of two large altars: that of the Trinity, to the left of the main door, and that of Our Lady, to the right. The first was described by Richa in 1757 as a projecting structure, with the *Doctors of the Church* surrounding the *Redeemer* on the baldachin. A document of 1404 records a payment of no less than 40 florins to Mariotto for the paintings. On the altar there was also an *Intercession* on canvas, now in the Metropolitan Museum, New York, attributed to Niccolò Gerini and to the Master of the Coronation of Christ Church: the subject was perhaps connected to the Plague. After the destruction of the altar the surviving quatrefoils (we do not know what happened to the other two) were placed in the Canons' Sacristy. On the altar of the Virgin, there were the four *Evangelists* by Lorenzo di Bicci and an *Agnus Dei* by Pesello; the altar also had an altarpiece by Mariotto di Nardo, and a highly venerated fresco of the Virgin 'full of graces'.

a typical example of the Byzantine style which dominated painting before the revolutionary innovations of Giotto; it has sometimes been attributed to the Florentine artist Coppo di Marcovaldo (ca. 1225-1280), Cimabue's predecessor and designer of some of the most beautiful mosaics in the Baptistery. The second image (facing the entrance) is certainly the work of Jacopo del Casentino, who flourished in the first half of the 14th century. The frame, and the support used for carrying the panel in procession, were added in the early 16th century.

On the entrance wall, to the left of the door, are displayed six wooden quatrefoils painted in tempera on a gold ground. The three on the left, starting from the top, show the Evangelists JOHN, MATTHEW and MARK (1398), 9 and are by Lorenzo di Bicci. Originally these paintings were inserted into the wooden baldachin above the altar of the Madonna delle Grazie, between the central and the right-hand door on the counter-façade of the Cathedral. In this arrangement the four Evangelists flanked the *Agnus Dei*, painted by Giuliano d'Arrigo known as Pesello, and now lost together with the *Luke* by Lorenzo.

The quatrefoils on the right show two DOCTORS OF THE 10 CHURCH and CHRIST (centre). They were painted in 1404 by Mariotto di Nardo for the wooden baldachin above the Trinity altar, which backed onto the counter-façade between the central and the left-hand door. The two other *Doctors* which flanked the image of Christ have been lost.

To the right of the door is a panel with ST CATHERINE OF 11
ALEXANDRIA AND SCENES FROM HER LIFE. The unusual structure
betrays the presence of later additions: the older portion,
dating from the second half of the 14th century, corresponds to the pointed panel and is probably by Giovanni
del Biondo. The balance of the composition is here somewhat disturbed by an excessive attention to detail. St Catherine is shown crowned in the centre, holding a book in
her right hand and the palm of martyrdom in her left; to
the right is the kneeling donor, identified by an inscription
below as Nòferi di Giovanni di Bartolomeo Bìscheri, an
eminent citizen who had been Consul of the Wool Guild
since 1378. The two portraits facing one another in the
foreground show Bartolomeo and Giovanni, sons of Nòferi, and were possibly added in the first half of the 15th
century by Giovanni del Ponte, the painter responsible for
the eight scenes at the sides. The scenes, from top to bottom and from left to right, show: the *Conversion of St Ca-*
therine, St Catherine and the philosophers, the Saint's mas-
ters burned alive, the *Visit of the empress Faustina and the*
general Porphyry to St Catherine in prison, the *Beheading*
of the empress, the *Saint before the emperor Maxentius* (or
Maximinus II Daia), the *Torture of the wheel* and the *Be-*
heading of the Saint. At the sides of the cusp Giovanni also painted the heads of St Bartholomew (left) and St John
(right), the name-saints of Nòferi's children. Although of
somewhat mediocre workmanship, this composite work
is of great historical and documentary interest. It comes
from the Cathedral, where in 1407 Nòferi, founded the
family chapel and obtained the right of burial there for
himself and his descendants.

Next there is a panel showing ST ZENOBIUS WITH A FEMALE 12
DONOR, surmounted by an Annunciation. The Florentine
Saint was painted in his bishop's mantle and mitre by Jacopo di Cione, the brother of Andrea and Nardo, in the
late 14th century.

An early 15th-century tempera of the BEHEADING OF THE 13
BAPTIST is at present in restoration. The type of support
(canvas on wood) and the fact that the image is so wasted
suggest that this painting was a standard to be carried in
processions. The treatment is remarkably naturalistic and
the work has traditionally been regarded as Florentine,
though some recent critics ascribe it to Antonio Veneziano's late period; it may be that the restoration, apparent-
ly a complex one, will cast some light on the problem of
attribution.

Above, JACOPO DI CIONE, *St Zenobius*
with a female donor (late 14th
century). The original location of
this panel is unknown, but it has
been associated with the Company
of St Zenobius, whose members
met regularly in Santa Reparata.
Below, the *Beheading of St John*
the Baptist (early 15th century),
attributed to ANTONIO VENEZIANO.
Opposite, GIOVANNI DEL BIONDO (with
later additions by GIOVANNI DEL
PONTE), *St Catherine of Alexandria*
and scenes from her life (last three
decades of the 14th century).

Immediately after the construction of the dome, a provisional wooden choir was set up in the Cathedral. A century later the wooden choir appeared not only inadequate but falling to pieces. Thus it was that in 1547 Cosimo I de' Medici commissioned from Baccio Bandinelli a monumental choir, which the sculptor designed in collaboration with Giuliano di Baccio d'Agnolo. Their project espoused the octagonal form of the old wooden choir, and involved a colonnade bearing an Ionic entablature richly decorated with coloured marbles and bronzes; no fewer than 300 reliefs were to be required. The execution of this monumental design proved to be much slower than expected, and the final appearance of the choir (completed in 1572) was quite different from the ambitious initial plan; in particular, the reliefs of the *Prophets* and *Apostles*, the work of Bandinelli himself and of his pupil Giovanni Bandini, were reduced to eighty-eight. But the sculptural decoration did not finish there: behind the high altar was a marble group showing *Adam and Eve* (the sculptor made two versions, one of which is now in the Boboli Gardens and the other in the Bargello); on the altar itself was a *Dead Christ* supported by an angel, with a second angel bearing the Symbols of the Passion; on the altar-steps, in the centre, stood the figure of *God the Father* (Bandinelli made two versions: one was transformed into a *Jupiter* and is now in the Boboli Gardens, whilst the other is in the first cloister of the church of Santa Croce).

This 16th-century arrangement of the choir was to change completely. In 1721 the *God the Father* was replaced by Michelangelo's *Bandini Pietà* (→ pp. 72-76), and from 1838 the architect Gaetano Baccani, as part of his overall purist approach – which tended to eliminate or minimise the presence in the Cathedral of those elements not in harmony with the gothic linearity of the interior –, simplified the octagonal enclosure, removing the colonnade and the reliefs which are now displayed in the Museum's Room of the Paintings.

The choir bas-reliefs

Low down on the end portions of the two long walls, and
on the short fourth wall (the one with the door leading
into the octagonal chapel) are twenty-four MARBLE BAS-RE-
LIEFS from the choir of the Cathedral (→ opposite page).
Their elegant style, like that of the other panels still in the
Cathedral, seems influenced by the paintings of the Florentine Mannerists.

The work of Bartolomeo Bandinelli (commonly known
as Baccio), these reliefs are an agreeable contrast to the in-
expressive and academic heaviness of other of his sculptures; the artist himself must have been proud of the result, because in the marble base of the statue of *God the
Father* he inserted his SELF-PORTRAIT in relief, signed and
dated MDLVI (1556), and now to be seen on the entrance
wall above the reliefs.

In the centre, the final object displayed in this room is a
BADALONE or lectern used to support the large liturgical
codices. This example, in carved wood and *pietre dure*,
was given to the Baptistery of San Giovanni by the Medici
family in the later 16th century.

*In the middle of the short left-hand wall of the Room of the
Paintings is the entrance to the little chapel built when the
Museum was restored in 1954.*

OPA

The Chapel was built in 1954 to contain some of the most precious relics of Santa Maria del Fiore. The documents dealing with payments and commissions for goldsmith's work destined for Cathedral, for the most part published by Poggi, are very numerous. The same can be said of the artists who worked in this field: their names are listed in the registers of the Silk Guild, which had its headquarters in Por Santa Maria and which from about 1320 accepted goldsmiths amongst its members. There is no lack of important sources, such as Giorgio Vasari's *Lives of the Artist* and the autobiography of Benvenuto Cellini (whose judgements on his rivals are frequently harsh). The problem for scholars is to relate the works to the authors. However, it is certain that the Opera del Duomo and the Opera di San Giovanni made use of a limited number of workshops, the best available, where they also sent pieces in need of restoration or refashioning. The latter practice survived into the 18th century, the early decades of which saw the feverish activity of Holzman.

7. The Chapel

In the small octagonal space are six reliquaries from the Cathedral (other reliquaries, most of them from the Baptistery, are in the Room of the Silver Altar: → pp. 128-138). These precious objects, which were displayed to the people on religious feasts, have in the past undergone many additions and alterations: in particular, in the early 18th century the silversmith Bernardo Holzman was commissioned to restore the entire Cathedral's precious-metal collection, and he remounted pieces from different periods. We describe them in the order they are found in the six glass cases, beginning as usual from the left.

RELIQUARY OF THE VEIL OF ST AGATHA AND OTHER SAINTS. This splendid object of silver, brass and gilded copper, embossed and with additions cast in the round, was finished in 1714. The Grand Ducal silversmith Bernardo Holzman put his great technical skills at the disposal of the designer of the piece, Giovan Battista Foggini, one of the most interesting artists of the Florentine Baroque. The absence of figures is more than compensated for by the fantasy and architectural flair with which the relics are divided and their identifying scrolls arranged. The holy relics enclosed in this object – made at the expense of an anonymous gentleman, no doubt Grand Duke Cosimo III himself – were part of the Chiaromonte donation (→ opposite page).

In the early 15th century the Cathedral possessed only the relics of St Zenobius and St Sebastian, and unlike the Baptistery could not boast a 'treasure' of gold and silver. During the Council of Florence (1439), just when the Wool Guild was actively seeking relics to place in the Cathedral so as to counter-balance the Baptistery's collection, there arrived in Florence Federico di Chiaromonte (or Chiaramonte), who passed himself off as the former abbot of two non-existent Benedictine monasteries (St Mary of Josophat, near Thessalonica, and St Mary of Berreto, on the island of Crete) and offered the Opera a substantial collection of relics accompanied by forged certificates of authentication (cardinals' rather than papal ones, since the latter were more difficult to forge). After hesitating for some time, on 27 August 1439 the Opera del Duomo accepted the generous 'donation', reciprocating it with a huge sum of money. The relics were placed in two chests of ivory and ebony, which have now vanished; as for the contents, one part of them was discovered a few years ago in the Cathedral's wardrobe, and is now in the Baptistery; another part is preserved in the Cross of the Passion (→ pp. 62-63); the largest part, however, is inside the reliquary of the veil of St Agatha (right). Made by BERNARDO HOLZMAN, the Opera's official goldsmith, to a design by Giovan Battista Foggini, the object was commissioned in 1710 by the Grand Duke Cosimo III and sealed in 1714. Foggini, the Grand Duke's favourite architect and a sculptor in the classical manner, united an undeniable virtuosity with a constant search for pure and elegant forms: here he succeeded in devising a solution to the problem of displaying the relics and their identifying labels that is both original (in its application to a reliquary) and in harmony with the taste of the age (it is the kind of decoration found on numerous baroque cabinets).

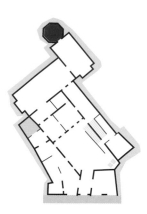

Above, the reliquary of the chains of St Peter; below, one of the three windows seen from behind. According to De Migliore the relic was given by the Countess Matilda; in reality it does not appear in the inventory of Santa Reparata drawn up in 1418, but it does appear in the list of relics acquired from the Chiaromonte donation (1439). On stylistic grounds we may suppose that the casket is earlier than the donation; it was probably meant for something else and was reused between 1566 (when the chains are mentioned elsewhere) and 1615, when Minerbetti described the present arrangement. The casket has few figures, unlike the reliquary of St Anthony Abbot (opposite), where in addition to the Baptist, St Zenobius and Pope St Victor we find also the Apostles Peter, Paul and Barnabas, St Sebastian and St Louis IX of France, patron saint of the Parte Guelfa.

RELIQUARY OF THE CHAINS OF ST PETER. This is a small 15th- 2 century casket of gilded copper, with some parts in embossed silver. The base of the reliquary rests on small lion's feet and is adorned with three lobed arches. The lion's feet, the engraved plate around the lid and the scroll inside the casket all probably date from the 18th century. The relic was donated in 1439 by Federico di Chiaromonte (→ p. 59).

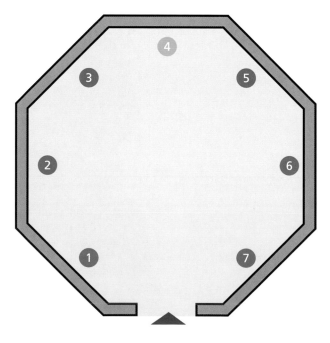

Right, the tempera panel of the *Madonna between St Catherine of Alexandria and St Zenobius* (1335), attributed to Bernardo Daddi; beneath the Virgin, the figures of one male and two female donors; in the pinnacle, Christ in benediction. On the step, between the names of the Saints is written the date 25 February 1334 (i.e. 1335, since the Florentine calendar began with the feast of the Annunciation on 25 March). The Madonna holds an open book displaying an invocation to the "Virgin Mary of Bagnuolo". The mention of this small village near the Impruneta (a few miles south of Florence) has suggested a connection with the Gherardini family, who were the local lords. Variously attributed, it has been ascribed to the school of Bernardo Daddi – or to Bernardo himself (Giulia Brunetti) – because of its miniaturist details (e.g. the little figures of the patrons, the Virgin's hands) typical of that artist. Below, Antonio di Salvi Salvucci, the reliquary of St Anthony Abbot.

Reliquary of St Anthony Abbot. Made between 1511 3 and 1514, it is attributed to Antonio di Salvi Salvucci, a pupil of Antonio del Pollaiolo, on the basis of its similarity to a work certainly by him, the *Banquet of Herod* on the right side of the Silver Altar (→ pp. 120-122). It was donated to the Cathedral in 1514 by the Parte Guelfa, which owned the patronage of a chapel dedicated to St Victor and St Anthony Abbot. Made of silver and gilded copper, it stands on a high stepped foot with two rows each of six enamels. On top of the short shaft, decorated with cornices, is a hexagonal *tempietto* with six windows: three of them are glazed with crystal, through which the relics can be seen, and three are filled with enamels representing the Baptist, St Zenobius and Pope St Victor; at the base of the *tempietto* are other enamels with Saints; above, a hexagon bears enamelled images of the Apostles; at the top, an onion-dome surmounted by a node supports the statue of St Anthony Abbot cast in silver.

The series of glass cases is interrupted by an altarpiece showing the Madonna between St Catherine and St Zeno- 4 bius; it is dated 25 February 1334 and is attributed to Bernardo Daddi, a follower of Giotto.

Below, the reliquary of St Jerome by Antonio di Salvi Salvucci, one of the most astonishing works of the late 15th century, although there are one or two stylistic lapses in the enamels (which in the upper series show scenes from the life of the Saint). The silver vessel supporting the relic of St Jerome's arm is encircled by a bone ring believed to have belonged to the Saint's girdle.

Above, one of the panels that decorate the base of the *tempietto*: the scene shows monks fleeing in terror, while the lion submissively offers his paw to St Jerome.

RELIQUARY OF ST JEROME, in embossed and gilded silver. 5 The large foot is decorated with two series of enamelled medallions showing episodes from the life of St Jerome; there are more enamels at the base of the hexagonal *tempietto*, whose arched windows allow us to see clearly the Saint's jaw-bone. On the hemispherical dome of the *tempietto* are two superimposed aedicules containing St Jerome's arm, ending with another dome surmounted by his statue cast in silver.

This impressive reliquary was made from 1487 in the workshop of the Florentine goldsmith Antonio di Salvi Salvucci; the relics were part of the Chiaromonte donation (→ p. 59).

RELIQUARY-CROSS OF THE PASSION OF CHRIST, in embossed 6 gold, with enamels and gem-stones. This splendid object, finished by the goldsmith Cosimo Merlini in 1618, was made for Grand Duke Cosimo II and his wife Maria Magdalena of Austria to replace an earlier reliquary in silver and crystal.

During the 17th century the Cross, frequently moved around and carried in processions, suffered some damage: in particular, the gems mounted on the external quadrilobes which conclude the arms of the Cross frequently became detached. The most radical restoration was carried out in the 18th century by Bernardo Holzman, who on that occasion also refashioned the voluted foot as we see it today.

The relics inside are especially interesting. The most important are the two small crosses inserted into the central roundel and the one surmounting the upper arm. The first – Byzantine work of the 11th or 12th century – consists of two fragments of the Cross of Christ mounted in gold filigree; at the intersection of the arms there is on one side a rectangular cameo showing Christ in benediction, on the other side an enamel of the same subject, and the initials of Jesus Christ in Greek letters (IC XC – corresponding to IS CI IS in our alphabet – for *Iesoûs Christós*). The second cross, which is smaller but presumably of the same period, is also of gold filigree, with gems at the extremities of the arms. Its inner compartment contains minute relics of the Passion of Christ: a fragment of bread consecrated at the Last Supper, a piece of the sponge offered by a Roman soldier to Christ on the Cross, a piece of the scarlet cloak in which Jesus was arrayed by his tormentors, a thorn from the crown placed on his head, and a piece of his tunic. Between

In the early 16th century Santa Maria del Fiore finally managed to overtake San Giovanni as regards the number and importance of commissions for reliquaries. In the space of a few years however both Treasures suffered severe losses: during the Siege of Florence by the emperor Charles V (1529-1530) many pieces had to be sacrificed to the city's defensive needs, and the flood of 1557 caused further irreparable losses. It was probably in order to deal with the resulting confusion that in 1615 Cosimo II ordered a *recognitio* of the relics, to be conducted by the archdeacon Cosimo Minerbetti. According to his report, an invaluable source of information on the relics, the Cross of the Passion (right) was being made during that year: it would be finished in 1618. In it was placed the wooden 'crosslet' donated (in reality, sold; but purchases are never referred to as such, they are always donations) in 1454 by Marco Chestialselim, until that time preserved in a now lost reliquary. The Cross also contains relics from the Chiaromonte donation, including a splinter from the Reed and a large piece of wood from the True Cross. The Bolognese Cosimo Merlini here goes back to the late 16th-century Medicean style (the names of Odoardo Vallet and Jacques Bylivelt come to mind), combining structural lightness with bright polychromy. In 1700 (the date of the base by Bernardo Holzman) an inventory was made of the jewels (among others, 120 pearls, 32 garnets, 11 Bohemian and Indian topazes, 6 emeralds, 4 amethysts, 2 aquamarines and 2 chalcedonies). The Cross used to be carried in procession on Good Friday, on 3 May (the Finding of the Cross) and on 14 September (the Exaltation of the Cross). In the 18th century it was exposed on the occasions of prayers for recovery during the illnesses of Ferdinando de' Medici and of Gian Gastone, the last Medici Grand Duke.

1454 and 1455 both of these small crosses were sold to the Cathedral by Marco 'Cristianselmo' (Chestialselim), one of the many Greeks who took refuge in Italy, and especially in Florence, after the capture of Constantinople by the Turks in 1453.

RELIQUARY OF THE FINGER OF ST JOHN THE BAPTIST. It contains 7 a relic donated by the Eastern emperor to Giovanni Corsini in 1391. On his return home, the Florentine nobleman gave the finger-bone to his brother Pietro, the Cardinal of Florence: the following year it was presented to the Chapel of St Laurence in the Cathedral, the patronage of which was held by the Corsini family. Of gilded silver, it was made in the second or third decade of the 15th century by Matteo di Giovanni, an assistant of Tommaso Ghiberti, although some parts may be older; a number of joins bear witness to later interventions; in 1707 Bernardo Holzman subjected it to an important restoration. The foot, disproportionately large in relation to the rest of the reliquary, makes one suspect a separate provenance; it is divided into six lobes, with enamels of St Zenobius between the deacons St Eugenius and St Crescentius, and of the Virgin between St Miniatus and St Reparata. The *zoccolo* is decorated with more enamels showing heads of prophets and scrolls. The slim shaft with three nodes supports the aedicule with its ampulla of rock-crystal containing the relic. This aedicule is formed by six twisted columns supporting trilobed arches surmounted by pinnacled pediments; from the dome rises a slim gothic spire.

We now return to the Room of the Old Façade and pass through the double-arched entrance to the Lapidarium.

8. The Lapidarium

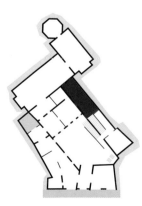

In this room are gathered architectural and sculptural fragments from the Cathedral, Baptistery and Campanile.

The numerous TOMB-STONES on the walls bear the names and often the coats of arms of many old Florentine families; they come from the cemetery which extended along the façade and south side of the old cathedral of Santa Reparata. They were discovered and moved to the deposits of the Opera on two separate occasions: in the 14th century, during the construction of the present cathedral, and in the later 19th century, when the present façade was built.

The font and the choir-enclosure from the Baptistery date from the 12th to 13th century. In 1577 they were dismantled by the Grand Duke's architect Bernardo Buontalenti, and the PANELS were reused on various Florentine buildings. We see a few of them on the left wall: some are rectangular, with rosettes on a ground of black marble in-

The original appearance of the old font has been reconstructed largely on the basis of the drawing made by Buontalenti before he destroyed it in preparation for the christening of Filippo, eldest child of Francesco de' Medici and Joanna of Austria: it was octagonal in form and was located at the altar in the scarsella.

On the basis of a famous and much-discussed passage in Dante's *Inferno*, where the poet describes an incident that took place in his "bel San Giovanni" (XIX, 16 ff.), and of contemporary illustrations to the *Divine Comedy*, it is thought that around the perimeter of the font there was a series a deep basins in which babies were immersed. The object of Buontalenti's demolition was to restore to the interior of the Baptistery its original 'Roman' sense of space, spoiled by the addition of the 13th-century font ("the fonts in the middle", wrote the learned Vincenzo Borghini, "distort it, and by occupying the central space make it appear half as big as it really is"). The stone panels were heaped up near the wall and it seems that the people carried off fragments to their houses, to preserve them as relics. The fragments displayed in the Museum are all the results of chance discoveries, the principal one being made in 1905, during work on the roof of the Baptistery. The characteristic dichrome intarsia decoration with portions in relief, of Pisan origin, dates from the 11th century. Right, ANDREA DELLA ROBBIA's lunette with *St Zenobius and two angels*. Opposite, the reliquary of the finger of St John the Baptist.

tarsia; others are square, and have rosettes framed by a roundel or a rhombus, on a ground of black and white marble intarsia.

At the end of the left wall, high up near the stairs, a lunette in glazed terracotta shows ST ZENOBIUS AND TWO ANGELS (1496), by Andrea della Robbia. The severe gravity of this piece, which stood over the door of the old Compagnia di San Zanobi, abolished in the 18th century, reflects the religious climate of Savonarola's Florence.

At the end of the right wall of the Lapidarium is a door leading to the old vestibule of the Opera's headquarters, now the Room of the Porta della Mandorla.

The Porta della Mandorla ('of the Almond') owes its name to the shape of the frame which encloses Nanni di Banco's *Assumption* in the pediment. In medieval art this particular shape, representing the light of glory, was often used to accompany the figure of the Virgin or of the transfigured Christ: in the first case, the almond also symbolised the Divine maternity, as a womb containing life; in the second, it alluded to Christ's Divine nature concealed beneath His humanity. The decoration of the door, begun in the 1370s, was not finished until the end of the following century (in the mean while the other three doors of the Cathedral had been completed: the Porta dei Cornacchini on the north side, the Porta del Campanile and the Porta dei Canonici on the south side): the long-drawn-out period of work on the door has allowed scholars clearly to discern in the reliefs the transition from the late-gothic (adopted by artists such as Giovanni d'Ambrogio, Piero di Giovanni Tedesco, Jacopo di Piero Guidi and Niccolò di Piero Lamberti) to early renaissance style. The splays of the door's pointed arch are decorated with small figures, plant motifs and angels; at the top there is a most beautiful *Pietà* (below, right), which scholars are uncertain whether to attribute to NANNI DI BANCO or to DONATELLO.

9. The Room of the Porta della Mandorla

This small room – which until the rearrangement of 1999-2000 was the bookshop and ticket office – displays the sculptural decoration from the *Porta della Mandorla*, the monumental doorway on the north side of the Cathedral, more of less opposite the present-day Via Ricàsoli, which takes its name from the *mandorla*, or almond, framing the relief above the pediment, a magnificent *Assumption of the Virgin* by Nanni di Banco.

In the centre of the room is a large SCULPTURAL FRAGMENT 1-5 from the splays of the ogival arch framing the lunette above the door. The reliefs, which date from the first decade of the 15th century, decorated the apex and the right-hand portion of the arch; they were removed and re-placed by copies during restoration work carried out be-

tween 1869 and 1871. The first on the left (the CHRIST from   1
the top of the arch) is of uncertain attribution: Donatello
has been suggested, but so too have Nanni di Banco and
other artists. There follow other figures (a PUTTO WITH A   2-5
SNAIL IN AN ACANTHUS BUSH, an ANGEL, a HERCULES IN AN ACAN-
THUS BUSH and another ANGEL) attributed to Niccolò di Pietro Lamberti.

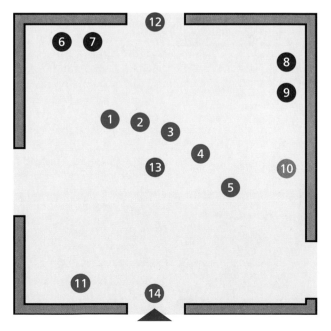

Above, the reliefs showing a *Putto
with a snail*, *Hercules* and an *Angel*,
by NICCOLÒ DI PIETRO LAMBERTI, come
from the right splay of the pointed
arch. Above, right, the pediment
of the Porta della Mandorla, with
the *Assumption* by NANNI DI BANCO.

On the right, the *Angel Gabriel* and the *Virgin Annunciate*, attributed to GIOVANNI D'AMBROGIO. It is thought that these statues were made around 1397, when the Porta della Mandorla was already completed in its lower portion. As the deliberations of the Operai for 1409 and 1414 bear witness, they were set up in the Cathedral while the lunette intended for them was being prepared. They were installed in 1414, but by July 1489 they had already been removed – a document refers to the problem of filling the "empty space over the door". In the end a mosaic was decided upon, and the group was replaced by the *Annunciation* by Domenico and David Ghirlandaio. The paternity of the statues – in which the gothic tradition is pervaded by a new interest in the antique – has been debated for over a century. An important breakthrough was made when it was realised that there are marked stylistic affinities between the group and the reliefs on the left splay of the door, suggesting a common authorship. Among the names proposed were Niccolò Lamberti, Jacopo di Piero Guidi, and especially Giovanni d'Ambrogio (whose workshop was certainly responsible for the reliefs) and Nanni di Banco or his father Antonio. On the basis of many clues, including a passage in Vasari's *Lives*, Brunetti has proposed attributing the group to the young Jacopo della Quercia. But the question remains open: it has recently been suggested, for example, that the figures were in fact sculpted in the 18th century by the workshop of Bernardo Cavaceppi (Bergstein). The statues, both in good state of preservation, are unfinished behind, where they have a metal ring and a cavity so that they can be attached to the wall; on the back of the *Angel* are two more cavities for attaching the wings. It is possible that in the left hand the *Angel* held a lily, the symbol of pure love and the traditional flower of Annunciations.

On the wall opposite the entrance, to the left of the door known as the Door of Audience, there is an ANGEL GABRIEL and a VIRGIN ANNUNCIATE (ca. 1397). We do not know for certain who made these two 14th-century statues: they have been attributed to the youthful Jacopo della Quercia, and to an otherwise unknown Master of the Annunciation, but are today assigned with greater probability to Giovanni d'Ambrogio. It is however certain that the group originally stood inside the Cathedral, on the altar of the Blessed Trinity; from there they were moved in 1414 to decorate the Porta della Mandorla until 1490, when they were removed and replaced by the mosaic of the *Annunciation* still *in situ*, the work of Domenico and David del Ghirlandaio. We notice that the *Virgin Annunciate* differs from the customary iconography in her hair, which is short like a boy's, or – perhaps more to the point – like a novice nun's.

On the wall to the right of the entrance are two statuettes of PROPHETS: they come from the pediment above the doorway of the Campanile, where they were set up in 1431, though they were made in 1406-1409. It is thought

The two *Prophets* (right), originally on the pinnacles at the sides of the Porta della Mandorla, were for a long time regarded as youthful works by Donatello, who at the time is known to have been working on the door. This hypothesis seemed to receive confirmation from a document that mentions two statuettes of prophets made by the sculptor in 1408, but many scholars now tend to believe that this refers to the two prophets from the entrance door to Giotto's Campanile, displayed in the Room of the Panels (→ p. 97). So the question is still open, also because stylistically the statues do not seem to be by the same artist. The first *Prophet* (left) has been attributed, as well as to DONATELLO (on account of its affinity with youthful works by him), to Bernardo Ciuffagni. For the second *Prophet* (right), the names of Luca della Robbia and, with more probability, of NANNI DI BANCO have been proposed. Below, the bust of Filippo Brunelleschi attributed to GIOVANNI BANDINI KNOWN AS DELL'OPERA. Scholars have long been uncertain regarding the authorship of the great architect's bust; the aedicule in *mischio* from Seravezza, on the other hand, is certainly by Bandini, who made extensive use of this particular kind of marble in the cathedral choir.

that they were originally intended for the Porta della Mandorla, where they surmounted the pinnacles either side of the tympanum. Their authorship is problematical: a contemporary document mentions two *profetini*, or "small prophets", made by Donatello in 1408, without specifying their destination; in fact the first *Prophet* might well be by the young Donatello, while the second seems more likely to be by Nanni di Banco.

Beside the prophets, in a classical aedicule set into the wall, the BUST OF FILIPPO BRUNELLESCHI by Giovanni Bandini (later 16th century) is one of the many tributes paid by the members of the Opera to the immortal architect of the dome. The face was probably modelled from Brunelleschi's death-mask, which can be seen in another room (→ p. 159). The inscription beneath, PHILIPPI BRVNELLESCHI FLORENTINI ARCHITECTI CELEBERRIMI EFFIGIES / OB. AN. SAL. MCCCCXLIIII ("The likeness of Filippo Brunelleschi, the very famous Florentine architect, [who] died in the year of Salvation 1444"), contains an error of dating, because we know for certain that the architect of the dome died in 1446.

Right, DONATELLO, *The Creation of Eve* (ca. 1410). Attributed in the past to Luca della Robbia and to Ghiberti and only recently restored to Donatello (who as a young man is known to have modelled "some scenes and ornaments in bas-relief" for the Medici family), this panel "represents the first attempt known to us to cover a terracotta sculpture with a ceramic glaze" (Bellandi) and is therefore the direct antecedent of Luca della Robbia's glazed terracottaware. Unfortunately the lead-based glaze – and successive *a freddo* ('cold') gilding – has almost entirely disappeared. Below, WORKSHOP OF ANDREA DELLA ROBBIA, *Agnus Dei* (1487). This is a new kind of coat of arms compared with the old style by Luca: the garland is more luxuriant, and lacks the traditional moulded cornice. The roundel is part of a series of furnishings commissioned from Andrea by the cathedral authorities. In addition to the two lunettes displayed in this room, the documents mention "two angels made for the church" (1482), possibly to be identified with two *kneeling Angels* in the Victoria and Albert Museum (Gentilini; *contra* Pope-Hennessy, who ascribes them to Giovanni della Robbia) and a lost wooden *Crucifix* with moveable arms (1491) – it must have been similar to the one on display in the Room of the Silver Altar (→ p. 117) – to be exposed in the Cathedral on Good Friday (indicating that the production of the family workshop was not limited to terracotta).

On the entrance wall, a hexagonal panel in glazed terracotta shows the CREATION OF EVE. This piece, which possibly decorated the front of a nuptial cassone or chest, dates from the first decade of the 15th century and betrays the influence of Lorenzo Ghiberti. If, as seems likely, it is by Donatello, we have confirmation that the young sculptor (mentioned in a document after 1404) was part of the team working on the north door of the Baptistery. The subject recurs on a panel from the Campanile (→ pp. 81-82) and on the Door of Paradise (→ p. 182).   11

There are three more glazed terracottas in this room. The roundel set into the centre of the ceiling, comes from the workshop of Andrea della Robbia and shows the AGNUS DEI, symbol of the Wool Guild, inside a polychrome garland of fruit and flowers (1487): as we have seen, in 1331 this powerful corporation assumed the patronage of the Opera, which thenceforth adopted its symbol.   13

The second one, also polychrome, is the lunette above the door facing the entrance: it shows GOD THE FATHER IN BENEDICTION BETWEEN TWO ANGELS, and is by Andrea della Robbia (1488). The surface is entirely two-dimensional, according to a technique devised by the head of the Della Robbia family, Luca, and used by him on the cornice of the Federighi tomb now in Santa Trìnita and in the Studiolo of Piero de' Medici inside Palazzo Medici Riccardi.   12

Above, ANDREA DELLA ROBBIA, *God the Father in benediction between two angels* (1488) and *Madonna and Child with two angels* (1489). The lunette with *God the Father* is an example of the "painting in majolica" so much appreciated by Leonardo. Vasari mentions that shortly before his death Luca della Robbia "had begun to make scenes and figures painted in the flat, some examples of which I saw at his house". On the basis of this passage the lunette had been attributed to Luca. A document of 7 January 1488 recording a payment of 31 *lire* and 10 *soldi* in favour of Andrea and Benedetto di Paolo for "the figures above the door of the audience chamber" has induced several scholars to attribute it to Andrea; however, this record of payment cannot be taken as definite proof of the attribution, since – as has indeed been pointed out – the Della Robbia workshop also fired works by other artists (Brunetti). The work has been seen in relation to the renewed interest in mosaic-work in the cathedral workshop (→ p. 142); of such work the new Della Robbia techniques "could be an effective surrogate" (Gentilini). The lunette 'painted in the flat' showing *St Francis between two angels* dates from the same period and was made for the chapel of the Villa Corniolo at Borgo San Lorenzo. The *Madonna* lunette was installed in September 1489. It is generally thought to be by Andrea or his workshop, although some critics (e.g. Maud Cruttwell) have detected the hand of the young Giovanni della Robbia.

The third terracotta is above the entrance door and has only two colours. The white figures of the MADONNA AND CHILD BETWEEN TWO ANGELS (1489), by Andrea della Robbia, stand out in relief against a blue ground. The subject is treated with the iconographic and stylistic characteristics typical of the Della Robbia workshop, as seen for example in the lunette from the monastery of the Cappucine (now in the Bargello), or in the altarpiece in the Rocca di Gradara Chapel in the Marches.

We now climb the first flight of stairs leading to the upper floor, and reach a circular space – rather cramped, and lacking natural light – where the Pietà del Duomo by Michelangelo Buonarroti, is provisionally displayed.

Opposite, the *Pietà del Duomo* by MICHELANGELO BUONARROTI. Sculpted by Michelangelo half a century after his *Vatican Pietà* (1501), this masterpiece was intended for the artist's own funerary chapel in the Roman basilica of Santa Maria Maggiore. Below, the *Pietà di Palestrina* (today in the Accademia) and the *Pietà Rondanini* (in the Sforza castle in Milan): this latter work is certainly by Michelangelo, whereas the attribution to him of the former, discovered in the Barberini Chapel in Palestrina, has been denied by many scholars.

10. The Pietà del Duomo

Our account of this late masterpiece of Michelangelo's, known as the PIETÀ DEL DUOMO or *Pietà Bandini*, must begin with a glance at the events which accompanied and succeeded its creation.

The death of his friend Vittoria Colonna, in 1547, cast the great artist into a black depression. Approaching his eightieth year, he reflected insistently on death, and fastened on one of the classic subjects of religious iconography: the Pietà, or the mourning of the dead Christ, a famous version of which he had sculpted as a young man (St Peter's, Rome). This was to be a new kind of Pietà, however, different from the traditional one (where the dead body of Jesus is supported by a group of angels or saints). Michelangelo deliberately confused the subject with those of the Deposition and the Burial. He created various designs and produced three sculptural groups: this one, which was the first; the *Pietà di Palestrina*, now in the Accademia in Florence; and the *Pietà Rondanini*, in the Museum of the Sforza Castle in Milan.

The sculpting of the *Pietà del Duomo*, intended by Michelangelo as his own funerary monument, began perhaps in 1547 and ended in 1555, when the artist decided to destroy it. There were two reasons for this decision, one technical and one psychological. In the first place the block of marble chosen for the group turned out to be full of impurities and extraordinarily hard, so that according to Giorgio Vasari it emitted showers of sparks when attacked with the chisel. Secondly, Michelangelo was sunk deep into one of the depressive crises which punctuated his life and which became more severe with advancing age. It is Vasari again who tells us how he visited the artist in his house one evening, and how Michelangelo dropped a lantern. Calling to his servant to bring a new one, he remarked: "I am so old that often Death tugs me by the cloak to make me go with her; this body of mine will fall one day just like this lantern, and the light of life will go out". Somewhat cattily Vasari supposes that the lantern was dropped on purpose, to hide the unfinished Pietà from the eyes of one who knew about art; but more probably it fell during a moment of profound distraction, which Michelangelo himself interpreted correctly.

Nothing is more irritating to a depressive than being urged into action. We know that the servant who brought the new lantern, a certain Urbino, was continually exhort-

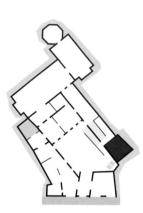

There has been much discussion as to the identity of the bearded figure supporting the dead Christ, to whom Michelangelo (judging from the surviving portraits) gave his own features. In the Gospels of Luke and of Mark it is Joseph of Arimathea – the disciple who took charge of the Holy Grail – who wrapped the dead body of Christ in fine linen and laid it in the sepulchre. The two biographers of Michelangelo – Condivi (1553) and Vasari (1568) – however, say that the figure is in fact Nicodemus, the Pharisee who in John's Gospel goes to visit Jesus at night, in secret, to question Him about His teaching. When Jesus tells him "Unless a man be born again, he cannot see the kingdom of God", Nicodemus asks, "How can a man be born when he is old?". The figure of Nicodemus is regarded as emblematic of those who observe the dominant institutional religion only exteriorly, whilst observing their own interiorly (religious dissimulation, or Nicodemism).

ing his master to finish the sculpture. One day, driven to distraction, Michelangelo snatched up a hammer and began hitting it in a rage, swearing never to finish it. At this point the Florentine Francesco Bandini, who was also a sculptor and an architect, managed to acquire it as it was, through the good offices of Tiberio Calcagni, one of the master's pupils. Calcagni himself restored the damaged portions, finished as well as he could the figure of the Magdalene, and carried out other small interventions on the group until he died.

The Pietà stood in Bandini's villa in Rome. Vasari pleaded in vain to have it sent to Florence for Michelangelo's tomb in Santa Croce. Only in the later 17th century did the Grand Duke Cosimo III manage to have it brought to the Tuscan capital. At first it stood in the Medici crypt in San Lorenzo, but in 1722 it was moved to the Cathedral. Since 1981 it has been in the Museum of the Opera, of which it is perhaps the greatest masterpiece.

Three figures stand around Christ: on his right the Magdalene, who occupies the place of honour traditionally assigned to the Virgin; in the centre, high up, Nicodemus, the converted Pharisee who assisted at the burial of Jesus, and to whom Michelangelo has lent his own facial features; on the left, the Virgin. The body of Christ, the cen-

tral element in the composition, slides downwards, with a movement which the artist has emphasised by the torsion of the bust and the broken line of the leg. The right arm, bent backwards, touches the shoulder of Mary Magdalene; the left, hanging inertly, fills the centre of the composition and continues the vertical of Nicodemus. This descending rhythm seems to be complemented and balanced by a circular, almost rotary movement from left to right. The profile of the tilted head of Jesus continues in the line of the bust and the thigh of the Virgin, follows with the right arm of the Magdalene, and concludes with the arm and shoulder of Christ. The left leg of Christ is missing. Grave as it is, this loss does not affect our appreciation of the compositional skill of the artist, who confers on the group a kind of inner spiritual animation, and has almost divested the marble of its material nature.

We now go up to the first floor. To the left and right of the stairs consoles support six HEADS *of uncertain provenance, some dating from Imperial Roman times, some from the 15th century.*

Passing through the door we enter the Room of the Cantorie. In order to follow a logical order – which we shall shortly explain – we advise you to cross it and pass through the door into the Room of the Panels from the Campanile.

11. The Room of the Panels from the Campanile

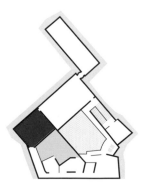

As we know, the designer and first architect of the Campanile was Giotto, who worked on its construction from 1334 until his death in 1337. The artist managed to complete only the lowest order, which has space for seven hexagonal panels each on the west, south and east sides; the north side had no panels because it was taken up by a walkway which, for the convenience of the clergy, connected the Campanile to the Cathedral. Following the en-

Between 1965 and 1967 the reliefs which decorated the first two orders of the Campanile were moved to the Museum and replaced by copies. The new arrangement has restored the original sequence, so that we can observe the relations between the two registers and within the individual registers. Filling the room is a large octagonal marble intarsia (above) from the Baptistery, where it was installed in the 18th century. Still there in the early 20th century (opposite, in a photograph of the period), it was removed during the restoration campaign conducted by the architect Giuseppe Castellucci to restore the Baptistery to its Romanesque appearance. On that occasion the baroque altar placed in the centre of the scarsella was also dismantled: the group by the sculptor Girolamo Ticciati which surmounted it, a marble *St John the Baptist in Glory* (1730), is now in the deposits of the Museum.

largement of the entrance doorway (1347-1348), two panels were removed from the east side and moved to the north side; the demolition of the walkway (1431) induced the Opera to commission five more panels from Luca della Robbia (1437-1439), so as to regularise the number to seven on this side as well. It should be noted that the original choice of seven for the four faces of the Campanile was far from accidental: in Biblical terms this number symbolised human perfectibility, and the subject of the reliefs is in fact mankind's march towards perfection.

Andrea Pisano, the master builder who continued the construction from 1337 to 1347, added onto Giotto's structure a second fascia decorated with lozenge-shaped panels (1337-1341), and built two further storeys with niches to receive statues. Andrea's successor Francesco Talenti completed the structure with the final three storeys, which have no sculptural decoration.

With their three superimposed registers – hexagonal panels, lozenges, statues – the images represent the story of mankind from the Creation to his first steps along the path of spirituality and of eternal salvation. The subject,

The first stone of the Campanile was laid on 18 July 1334. Building-work was then directed by Giotto, whom Giovanni Villani calls "the most sovereign master in painting who was to be found in his time", by then so celebrated as to obscure (said Dante) the fame of his master Cimabue. The painter retained the polychromy chosen by Arnolfo for the Cathedral, but did not employ mosaic. The result of a tremendous technical and financial effort, the construction was completed in 1359. This undertaking reflected the city's power and prosperity: at a time when Paris counted 80,000 inhabitants and Rome was little more than a country village, with over 100,000 inhabitants Florence was one of the greatest cities of Christendom, and intended to celebrate the civilisation of which it was an expression by narrating the destiny of man in a "theology of work" (Paolucci). Crucial for the understanding of the iconographic scheme (54 reliefs and 16 statues) was the work of Julius von Schlosser (1896), who studied its relations with Scholastic doctrines, tracing its sources in medieval encyclopaedias.

developed in accordance with the tenets of Scholastic philosophy, was frequently treated on the façades of the gothic cathedrals of Northern Europe, but its application to a bell-tower is unique in the history of western art.

The present arrangement follows the original scheme of the first two rows, with the hexagonal panels below and the lozenges above. Our visit, too, follows the sequence of the Campanile (west, south, east and north sides).

The hexagonal panels

We begin with the hexagonal panels. Apart from the case of the last five panels, which are certainly by Luca della Robbia, the problem of attributions is exceedingly thorny; but we should remember that in medieval workshops the craftsmen worked in a spirit of collaboration and togetherness that assigned little importance to the entirely modern concern for artistic paternity. In the early panels inspired by Genesis some have detected a gothic flavour not wholly in tune with the art of Andrea Pisano, while the *Tubalcain*, the *Daedalus*, the *Navigation* and the *Agriculture* are seen to possess a sense of volume and an expressive tension derived from the example of Giotto. Some of the references to classical antiquity (such as the Hercules and Cacus in *Social Justice* or Phidias in *Sculpture*), while undoubtedly taken from medieval encyclopaedias, clearly foreshadow subjects which were to be widely employed in the Renaissance.

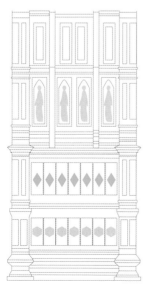

The iconographic cycles of the three buildings that form Florence's religious complex (Baptistery, Cathedral and Campanile) are all centred on the theme of Salvation. The Baptistery mosaics provide a kind of grandiose summary of the theme, from Genesis to the Last Judgement by way of the preaching of the Baptist and the life of Christ. The sculptural decoration envisaged by Arnolfo di Cambio for the façade of the Cathedral, on the other hand, concentrates "with dramatic clarity" (Verdon) on the figure of Mary and on the announcement of the good news. In the reliefs of the Campanile the accent is placed on man, and on his slow and weary journey towards civilisation and faith. Medieval thought subdivided human activities into three great classes: *Necessitas*, comprising the mechanical or manual arts, which are necessary to survival and seek to dominate nature; *Virtus*, the sphere of the values forming the basis of social organisation (family, city, state); *Sapientia*, which is the domain of intellectual activity and includes the Liberal Arts of the *Trivium* and *Quadrivium*, directed by the Theological and Cardinal Virtues. The history of civilisation opens on the west side with the celebration of divine operosity (the creation of man and of woman), and continues with the work of our first parents and the "discoverers of arts" (as Ghiberti called them), without pausing for episodes such as the temptation or the expulsion from Eden. A passage written by Ghiberti in his *Commentaries*, mentioning the "most beautiful measures" prepared by Giotto for the reliefs gave rise to a centuries-long debate on the role played by the master in the production of the reliefs. The problem was not merely one of attribution: to ascertain the extent of Giotto's contribution meant reconstructing the stages in the artistic development of Andrea Pisano, whose only certain work is the South door of the Baptistery.

1

The first panels narrate the early history of mankind according to the book of Genesis, and the discovery of the 'mechanical arts' as related in biblical tradition and in classical mythology. We begin at the wall with the door by which we entered. Starting from the left, seven panels from the west side of the Campanile show: 1. the CREATION OF ADAM (Gen 1:26); 2. the CREATION OF EVE (Gen 2:27); 3. the LABOURS OF OUR FIRST PARENTS, with Adam breaking the earth with a mattock as Eve wields a distaff (Gen 3:23); 4. JABAL, the inventor of animal husbandry, "the father of such as dwell in tents" (Gen 4: 20), sitting cross-legged in his tent surrounded by flocks; 5. JUBAL, "the father of them that play upon the harp and the organs" (Gen 4:21), the inventor of music; 6. TUBALCAIN, the first blacksmith, "a hammerer and artificer of every work of brass and iron" (Gen 4:22), shown at his anvil; 7. NOAH, the first farmer, who "began to till the ground, and planted a vineyard" (Gen 9:20). Attributions: 1-4 and 6 to Andrea Pisano; 5 to Nino Pisano; 7 to an assistant of Andrea.

There follow the panels from the south side: 8. GIONITUS, inventor of *Astronomy* (Brunetto Latini, *Trésor* I 21); 9.

2

3

4

5

6

7

9

10

11

12

13

14

At the end of the 19th century Andrea Pisano became the focus of intense interest. While toning down the emphasis of Vasari (who was inclined to attribute to him much more than his due), scholars began to regard him as the founder of a school. The collaboration between Giotto, whose "subtle pictorialism" was stressed, and Andrea, who appeared to be characterised by an intense sculptural concentration, was credited with the overcoming of gothic conceptualism and with the conquest of chiaroscuro as an element in the definition of space. According to Von Schlosser, Giotto restricted himself to outlining the Genesis episodes, which were later executed by the author of the *Planets*, the "most expert assistant" now identified as Nino Pisano. But not everyone has accepted this redefining of Giotto's role: there are some who attribute to him the reliefs of the second series as well. In order to explain the considerable stylistic differences between the reliefs (some of them gothic, others more 'classical' and mature), it has been supposed that work took place in two distinct phases (1334-1337 and 1342-1343). Becherucci advanced the theory that Andrea Pisano returned to Florence after the Black Death of 1348. His sudden departure from Florence in 1343 would have been due to the strong criticisms he received for having 'lightened' the Campanile vertically, departing from Giotto's design, but also to political reasons: in 1343 Walter of Brienne, for whom Andrea had designed fortifications, was driven out of Florence. We know that after 1343 Andrea worked in Pisa and then in Orvieto; but since from 1349 the documents record his son Nino as head of building works there, it is possible that he had returned in the mean time to Florence, where Vasari says that he was buried. This theory is today regarded as not very plausible, as in 1346 Francesco Talenti seems in charge of the cathedral works.

8

the ART OF BUILDING, or of scaffolding (Isidore of Seville, *Origines* XIX 20-23); 10. MEDICINE, with a physician seated on a cathedra inspecting a sample of urine, according to an iconographic convention which would last into the 17th century; 11. HUNTING, or simply HORSE-RIDING, symbolised by a horseman throwing a stone (Isidore of Seville, *Origines* XX 16); 12. WOOL-WORKING, or weaving (Isidore of Seville, *Origines* XIX 19-23); 13. *Legislation*, personified by PHORONEUS, the mythical Greek king of Argos (Brunetto Latini, *Trésor* I 17); 14. DAEDALUS, inventor of flight and personification of *téchne*, which for the Greeks was a combination of art and technology (Isidore of Seville, *Origines* XIX 8). Attributions: 8 and 9 to assistants of Andrea; 11, 12 and 14 to Andrea; 10 and 13 to Nino.

In its final arrangement the east side of the Campanile was decorated with five panels: 15. NAVIGATION (Isidore of Seville, *Origines* XIX 1-5); 16. SOCIAL JUSTICE, or the liberation of the earth from monsters, personified by Hercules who has just slain the cattle-thief Cacus (a frequent subject in medieval iconography); 17. *Agriculture*, or HOMO-GIRUS (Isidore of Seville, *Origines* XXVII 1); 18. THEATRI-

As we have seen (→ p. 79), it was von Schossler who discovered the sources of the Campanile's complex iconographic scheme by studying the medieval thinkers. The oldest source is undoubtedly Isidore of Seville, last of the Church Fathers, who lived between the 6th and 7th century. His best-known work is the *Etymologiae*, an encyclopaedia of all human knowledge, complete with glossary, which enjoyed an enormous success and provided an in-depth treatment of the Liberal Arts and their applications. More recent and equally well-known were *Li Livres dou Trésor*, a summa of medieval learning gathered by Brunetto Latini (ca. 1220-1294), the Florentine Chancellor so highly esteemed by Dante – who however places him in Hell, among the sodomites – and called by Giovanni Villani "the commencer and master in rough-hewing the Florentines". Another possible source is the *Speculum* in three parts (*naturale*, *doctrinale* and *historiale*; a fourth – *S. morale* – was added in the 14th century) which Vincent of Beauvais (1190?-1264) dedicated to Louis IX. The suggestion has been made that the arrangement of the reliefs faithfully reflects the divisions of this work: the first labours and the planets on the west side (*naturale*), the arts and virtues on the south side (*morale*), the Liberal Arts on the east side (*doctrinale*), and the *Prophets* and *Sibyls* on the higher order (*historiale*). Also worthy of note is Verdon's proposal that the cycle may have been inspired by a Dominican friar of Santa Maria Novella, Remigio, who had been a pupil of Thomas Aquinas. Quite apart from these learned references, however, the apologia for manual work reflects the myriad activities of the hard-working city, with its textile plants and building-sites. The incarnation of this bracing sense of euphoria is Hercules, the symbol of man's triumph over hostile nature, which seeks in vain to halt his march towards civilisation.

CA, or the *Art of festivals and spectacles*, represented by a chariot in allusion to the games of the circus (Isidore of Seville, *Etymologiae* XVIII 15-68; Vincent of Beauvais, *Speculum doctrinale*, XI 92); 19. ARCHITECTURE, where Euclid is shown drawing. Attributions: 15, 16 and 17 to Andrea; 18 and 19 to Nino.

WEST SIDE (THE SIDE OF THE CATHEDRAL FAÇADE)

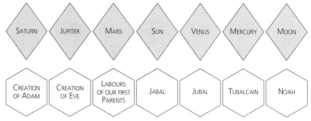

SATURN | JUPITER | MARS | SUN | VENUS | MERCURY | MOON

CREATION OF ADAM | CREATION OF EVE | LABOURS OF OUR FIRST PARENTS | JABAL | JUBAL | TUBALCAIN | NOAH

SOUTH SIDE (FACING TOWARDS VIA DE' CALZAIOLI)

FAITH | CHARITY | HOPE | PRUDENCE | JUSTICE | TEMPERANCE | FORTITUDE

ASTRONOMY | ART OF BUILDING | MEDICINE | HUNTING OR HORSE-RIDING | WEAVING | LEGISLATION | DAEDALUS

EAST SIDE (THE SIDE OF THE ENTRANCE DOOR)

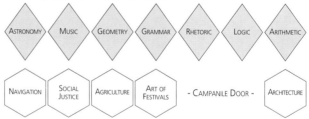

ASTRONOMY | MUSIC | GEOMETRY | GRAMMAR | RHETORIC | LOGIC | ARITHMETIC

NAVIGATION | SOCIAL JUSTICE | AGRICULTURE | ART OF FESTIVALS | - CAMPANILE DOOR - | ARCHITECTURE

NORTH SIDE (FACING TOWARDS VIA DELLA MORTA)

BAPTISM | CONFESSION | MATRIMONY | HOLY ORDER | CONFIRMATION | EUCHARIST | EXTREME UNCTION

SCULPTURE | PAINTING | ASTROLOGY (HARMONY) | GRAMMAR | LOGIC & DIALECTIC | MUSIC (POETRY) | GEOMETRY & ARITHMETIC

15

16

17

18

19

21

22

23

24

25

26

Originally the Campanile and the Cathedral were connected by a raised passageway. The narrow space between the two buildings was known as the Via della Morta: according to legend it was haunted by the ghost of the noblewoman Ginevra degli Almieri, who in 1396 had risen from her tomb inside the Cathedral. On the north side the lower order was undecorated, possibly because it was shaded by the passageway; it had only the reliefs of *Sculpture* and *Painting*, removed from the east side during work on the Campanile's entrance. In these reliefs, characterised by the intense and sculptural chiaroscuro typical of ANDREA PISANO's maturity, Luisa Becherucci has discerned an early example of the idea, which Michelangelo was to make his own, of "a form struggling to free itself with mortal effort from the imprisoning block of marble". The relief of *Sculpture* contains realistic representations of several tools in use at the time: hammer and chisel, tongs, double-pointed trimmer, drill. When it was decided to remove the passageway, LUCA DELLA ROBBIA was commissioned to make five more hexagons to complete the series. The subject of these reliefs remains uncertain. In reliefs 23 (*Grammar*, where the open door indicates the introductory nature of the discipline) and 24 (where the figures of the disputants are often compared with the very lively ones on Donatello's bronze doors in the Old Sacristy at San Lorenzo) would represent two of the arts of the *Trivium*. To complete the cycle of 'discoverers' of the Liberal Arts, the remaining reliefs would represent the arts of the *Quadrivium*. 25 (Orpheus, representing *Music*) and 26 (*Arithmetic* and *Geometry*) present no difficulties, while the interpretation of relief 22 is more complex, as we should expect to find *Astronomy*; and in fact Vasari interpreted the seated figure as Ptolemy, who is listening to the harmony of the celestial spheres.

20

On the north side there were the following panels (the first two were moved there from the east side in 1347-1348): 20. *Sculpture*, with the great Greek sculptor PHIDIAS intent on carving a nude; 21. *Painting*, showing the Greek painter APELLES; 22. *Harmony*, with the biblical blacksmith Tubalcain striking notes from his anvil (according to others, PTOLEMY, the father of *Astrology*); 23. *Grammar*, with a Latin scholar – PRISCIAN or Donatus – teaching two boys; 24. *Logic* and *Dialectic* (or *Philosophy*) represented by PLATO AND ARISTOTLE engaged in discussion; 25. *Music* (or *Poetry*) showing ORPHEUS taming the animals by improvising verses while playing his lute; 26. *Geometry and Arithmetic*, with EUCLID AND PYTHAGORAS. Attributions: 20 to Andrea; 21 to Nino. 22-26 are by Luca della Robbia.

The lozenges

The lozenge-shaped panels, where the marble figures stand out on a background of blue majolica, belong to the school of Andrea Pisano. The subjects shown here are the PLANETS, symbols of cosmic forces; the VIRTUES, representing the moral forces; the LIBERAL ARTS, as expressions of intellectual forces; and the SACRAMENTS, the means of salvation for souls.

The Campanile's second register was decorated with marble high reliefs on a background of blue majolica, divided into four series showing the *Planets* (west side), the *Virtues* (south side), the *Liberal Arts* (east side) and the *Sacraments* (north side). The first reference to the "seven planets" was made by Ghiberti in his *Commentaries*; Von Schlosser called them the elemental forces which, together with the moral faculties (Virtues) and the spiritual ones (Arts), direct man on his journey beyond the realm of mere necessity. The scheme of the reliefs follows the one traced in the 2nd century AD by the Greek scientist Ptolemy in his *Almagest*: this treatise, whose influence lasted into the 17th century, reached Europe in the 13th century, when it was translated into Latin from Arabic, the language in which it had enjoyed immense success. In the representation there are some original elements: *Jupiter*, for example, is here dressed as a monk, to symbolise the Divine wisdom. For centuries astronomy, astrology and mathematics formed a single discipline with the dignity of a science. It was believed that the planets exercised precise and inevitable influences, not only on the weather and on agriculture, but on the destinies of men: this opinion was opposed by Dante in *Purgatorio* XVI, where he follows Thomas Aquinas in asserting that the planets announce future events without predetermining them. In the 19th century the reliefs, which Vasari had attributed to Andrea, were associated with the style of Orcagna. The first four planets, "a stylistically homogeneous group, of marked originality" (Kreytenberg), have been ascribed to a single artist, called the MASTER OF SATURN. The relations between this series of lozenges and the hexagons beneath are to be regarded as chance ones, although there are compositional similarities: the *Sun*, for example, is shown frontally like *Jabal*.

1

Following the same order as for the hexagonal panels (i.e. beginning with the entrance wall and proceeding from left to right), we begin with the seven lozenges from the west side of the Campanile, representing the celestial bodies known to ancient and medieval astronomy: 1. SATURN, with the wheel of time; 2. JUPITER, here shown in the Christian guise of a monk with chalice and cross, symbols of the Faith; 3. MARS, shown as a mounted warrior; 4. the SUN, personified by Apollo, a young man crowned, holding a sceptre and the solar disk; 5. VENUS, supporting a pair of lovers with her right hand; 6. MERCURY, with the zodiacal sign of Gemini; 7. the MOON, seated on the waters (in allusion to her influence over the tides), holding a fountain in her right hand. Attributions: 1-4 to an assistant of Andrea known as the Master of Saturn; 5 and 6 to Nino Pisano; 7 to another assistant of Andrea known as the Master of the Moon.

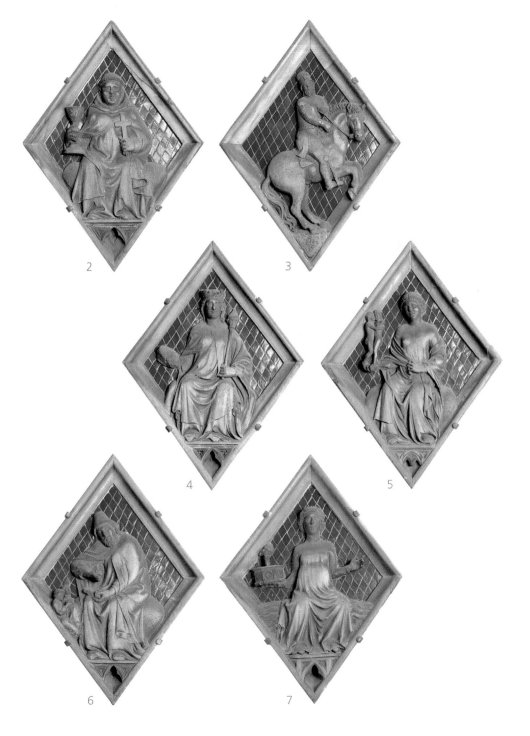

2

3

4

5

6

7

The celebration of human activities continues with the representation of the *Virtues*: the Theological ones (*Faith, Hope* and *Charity*) and the Cardinal ones (*Prudence, Justice, Temperance* and *Fortitude*). In the 1380s the two canonical sets of *Virtues* will be represented on the Loggia della Signoria (later known as Loggia dei Lanzi) next to the Palazzo Vecchio, in large quatrefoils with grounds of blue enamel; on another side of the same piazza, the Tribunale di Mercatanzia was beautifully decorated with the coats of arms of all the city guilds. The Divine plan which informs the history of civilisation makes use of the Virtues as guides to accompany man on his journey towards the kingdom of Grace, proclaimed by the statues in the upper order, the *Sibyls, Kings* and *Prophets* (Verdon). On this side the references between lozenges and hexagons seem more coherent: the astrologer appears to glance at the representation of *Faith*; the work on the building-site (a collective undertaking, although the figure of the *capomaestro* who directs the site is gradually emerging from his medieval anonymity) corresponds to *Charity*, supporting the weak; *Medicine* is related to *Hope*; *Prudence* seems to restrain the galloping horseman; the work of the weaver is surveyed by *Justice*; *Temperance* presides to the work of the legislator; the figure of Daedalus corresponds to *Fortitude*. The two series of reliefs were placed on the south side of the Campanile and therefore overlooked Corso Adimari (now Via Calzaioli), which was crowded with weavers' shops. Lozenges 9, 10 and 14 form a group of works by the so-called MASTER OF THE MOON, the sculptor of the last lozenge in the series of the *Planets*: in these reliefs, as has been observed by Gert Kreytenberg, "the sculptural articulation makes the figures stand out boldly from the background, which accentuates the tendency towards contrast by means of the blue majolica".

Next come the lozenges from the south side, showing the three Theological and the four Cardinal Virtues: 8. FAITH, with cross and chalice; 9. CHARITY, holding a heart in her right hand and a cornucopia in her left; 10. HOPE, with her wings spread and her hands joined in prayer; 11. PRUDENCE, with two heads (one old and one young), a serpent and a looking-glass; 12. JUSTICE, with sword and scales; 13. TEMPERANCE, pouring water into her wine; 14. FORTITUDE, wrapped in a lion's skin, with club and shield. Attributions: 8 to Gino Micheli da Castello; 9, 10 and 14 to an assistant of Andrea, probably the same who made 7; 11 and 12 to the maker of the hexagonal panel 9, called the Master of the Scaffolding (→ pp. 82-83); 13 to the Master of Saturn.

The lozenges from the east side show the seven Liberal Arts: 15. ASTRONOMY, holding an astrolabe; 16. MUSIC, with a psaltery; 17. GEOMETRY, with a book and compasses; 18.

8

The seven *Virtues* on the south side are followed on the east side by the seven *Liberal Arts*, what today we would call the humanities and the sciences. The *Chronicle* of Matteo and Filippo Villani (1, 10: "How the *Studium* first began in Florence") relates how after the plague of 1348 the Comune decided to institute the *Studium Florentinum*, the University of Florence, so as to attract foreigners, give lustre to the city and turn its inhabitants into "scientists and students of virtue". "Copious in every art and trade", Florence spared no expense, summoning all the most celebrated doctors "in all the faculties of sciences and of law", who "began to read on VI of the month of November, in the year of Christ MCCCXLVIII". In 1349 the city was proud to receive the Church's official approval from Pope Clement VI in Avignon, a privilege which not even the oldest and most famous universities had so far obtained: the pope "with his cardinals graciously received the request of our Comune, and considering that the city of Florence is the right arm of Holy Church... conceded us the privilege, that in the city of Florence doctorates may be taken, and theology be taught, and the sciences generally in all the other faculties. And the said *Studium* was endowed with all the benefits and honours granted by Holy Church, much more so than Paris or Bologna, or any other Christian city". A solemn ceremony was held in the Cathedral in honour of the very first Bachelor of Arts. It seems that the positioning of the reliefs illustrating the *Liberal Arts* was not random: the east side of the Campanile, in fact, faces towards Via dello Studio (Verdon). Reliefs 16, 18, 20 and 21 form, together with the lozenges of *Faith* and *Matrimony*, a homogeneous group: the schematic style which distinguishes it has been referred to GINO MICHELI DA CASTELLO, a sculptor well attested in Florence.

15

GRAMMAR, holding a scourge, and teaching three little boys; 19. RHETORIC, with sword and shield; 20. LOGIC, with shears; 21. ARITHMETIC, shown counting. Attributions: 15 to an assistant of Andrea identifiable as the maker of the hexagonal panel 7 (Master of Noah); 16, 18, 20 and 21 to Gino Micheli da Castello; 17 and 19 to Andrea.

Next come the lozenges from the north side, which show the Seven Sacraments. Formerly attributed to Alberto Arnoldi, a pupil of Andrea Pisano, these panels are now thought more probably to be by the painter and sculptor Maso di Banco, a follower of Giotto best known for the frescoes in the Bardi di Vernio Chapel in the basilica of Santa Croce, painted around 1340. (The only possible exception is 24, *Matrimony*, now thought to be by Gino Micheli da Castello.)

The seven sacraments are represented not allegorically but realistically; the symbolic aspects are merely hint-

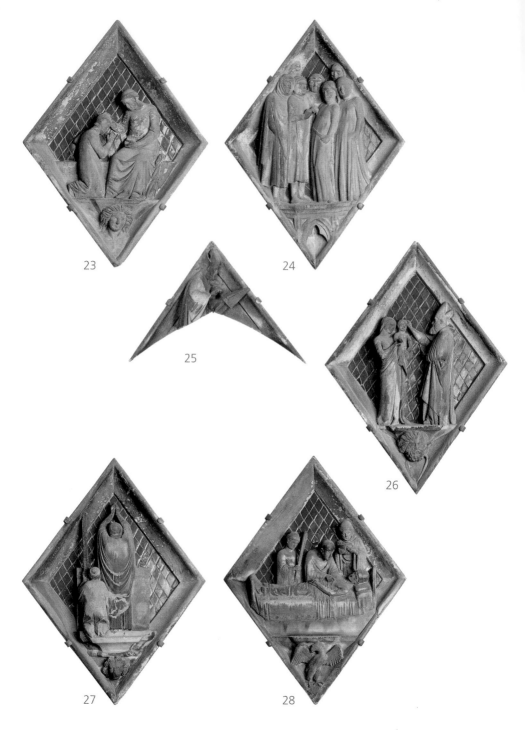

23

24

25

26

27

28

The series of lozenges on the north side of the Campanile is interrupted by the door which used to open onto the passageway leading to the Cathedral. The lunette over this door was adorned with a *Madonna and Child* surmounted by a cusp.

Lorenzo Ghiberti, followed by Vasari, erroneously identified this series as the "Seven Works of Mercy"; it was Forster, in 1835, who correctly identified the reliefs as the *Sacraments*. In the late 19th century Von Schlosser rightly recognised the relief sculpted in the cusp (formerly thought to represent *Penance*) as the figure of a bishop reading the formula of ordination over an ordinand (*Holy Order*). A hypothetical attempt to explain the meaning of the figures in the lower portion of the reliefs was made in 1906 by Venturi. The history of civilisation related on the sides of the Campanile reached its conclusion with the evocation of the kingdom of Grace, whose 'instruments' are here illustrated, deliberately situated on the side visible to the clergy who made use of the passageway. The lively figures in this cycle "stand out materially and optically from the background in neat fashion, offering themselves to the spectator as free sculptural groups": the individual personages are characterised by completeness of line, roundness of form and compactness of volume. Luisa Becherucci attributed the cycle to Alberto Arnoldi, a collaborator of Francesco Talenti, on the basis of a comparison with works made by him in the oratory of the Bigallo (1359-1364). But today it is generally thought that the series (apart from the relief representing *Matrimony*, by GINO MICHELI DA CASTELLO) was sculpted by MASO DI BANCO: although best known as a painter, according to Ghiberti he was "most noble and very gifted in one art and in the other" and "sculpted marvellously in marble". Neither of these theories has thus far received documentary support.

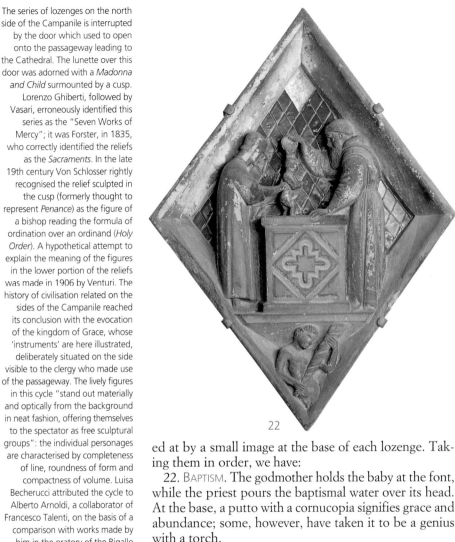

22

ed at by a small image at the base of each lozenge. Taking them in order, we have:

22. BAPTISM. The godmother holds the baby at the font, while the priest pours the baptismal water over its head. At the base, a putto with a cornucopia signifies grace and abundance; some, however, have taken it to be a genius with a torch.

23. CONFESSION, or PENANCE. A penitent kneels before a seated priest, who places his hand on him in sign of absolution. At the base, the head of a Fury, a symbol of the disorder of soul caused by sin.

24. MATRIMONY. The groom places the ring on the bride's finger; the priest stands in the centre, and four other people in the background – witnesses and relations. The trilobed ogival arch at the base, although present on other lozenges, has been taken by some as a reference to the solidity of conjugal union.

The elegant *Madonna and Child* (above) which occupied the lunette over the door on the north side of the Campanile is attributed to ANDREA PISANO: in this phase of his artistic development, before his 'chiaroscuro' period, the sculptor made innovative use of the French gothic forms he had learned during his training as a goldsmith (Luisa Becherucci). A plaster copy of the lunette, now in Berlin, is attributed to Alberto Arnoldi, at one time regarded as author of both works. Here and in the other lozenges from the Campanile the blue of the majolica ground was obtained from copper sulphate, and not from the cobalt oxide used by Luca della Robbia and his workshop for their famous glazed terracottas.

25. HOLY ORDER. Specially shaped to go above the lunette over the old north door of the Campanile, this relief shows the bishop reading the formula of consecration over the ordinand.

26. CONFIRMATION. A mitred bishop anoints the forehead of a child held in the arms of its godmother. At the base, a head of Hercules, symbol of investiture as a 'soldier of Christ' conferred by the sacrament.

27. THE EUCHARIST. This lozenge depicts the priest elevating the Host. He is assisted by an acolyte, kneeling at his left. At the base, a lion's head, symbol of the Church's supernatural strength.

28. EXTREME UNCTION. A skeletal invalid lies on his deathbed, as the priest anoints his breast. An acolyte reads the prayers for the dying while another holds a candle. At the base is an eagle, possibly a symbol of the soul's flight towards heavenly bliss.

The sculptural decoration on the three lower orders of the Campanile (hexagons, lozenges, statues) has for a long time been subjected to a campaign of intensive cleaning and restoration, whose results can be admired in the reliefs of *Painting* and *Sculpture* (→ pp. 86-87). The decision to remove the reliefs from the context for which they were designed, and relocate them in the Museum, gave rise to considerable controversy. However, numerous photographs taken over the years testify to the progressive and deleterious action of atmospheric agents on the reliefs: the calcium carbonate in the reliefs combines with the sulphur dioxide present in the atmosphere to produce calcium sulphate, and causes a process of gessification. This reaction, known as sulphatisation (or 'cancer') of marble, was already taking place in the early 20th century; the statues were therefore replaced by copies. Today, casts are generally preferred to copies: those of the Campanile reliefs were made by Andrea Rothe out of cement, pigment and marble dust, a technique now superseded by the use of synthetic resins. Above, the two *Prophets* and the *Redeemer* which decorated the door to the Campanile (below). On the following pages, *St Reparata* and the *Redeemer* by ANDREA PISANO.

As we have seen, all the lozenges from the north side are today assigned to Maso di Banco, except for 24, which is attributed to Gino Micheli da Castello.

The lunette and the other pieces of sculpture

Between the *Matrimony* and the *Confirmation* and beneath the relief of *Holy Order* there is a 14th-century ogival lunette showing, on the usual blue majolica ground, an image in relief of the MADONNA AND CHILD. It is probably by Andrea Pisano, and stood above the small raised door reached by the walkway connecting the Cathedral to the Campanile.

Immediately to the right of the entrance, on a pedestal, we see two marble statuettes representing CHRIST THE REDEEMER and ST REPARATA (ca. 1340), by Andrea Pisano. According to the documents these pieces were already in the vestibule of the Casa dell'Opera in 1870, but their original location is unknown; they may have stood on the pinnacles of one of the doors of the Cathedral.

On the opposite side of the room, also on a pedestal, are three other marble statuettes which stood on the pinnacles of the door to the Campanile. The two very fine PROPHETS at the sides have recently been attributed to Donatello and perhaps date from 1410, when the young artist was an apprentice in Ghiberti's workshop; the central statuette of the REDEEMER, of not outstanding quality, is attributed to the workshop of Francesco Talenti.

12. The Room of the Cantorie

We return now to the Room of the Cantorie, and position ourselves facing the entrance from the stairs. So as to follow the sequence dictated by the iconography of the Campanile we begin with the sixteen statues which stood in the niches on its third order. They were transferred to the Museum in 1937, when their long exposure to the elements had already caused considerable damage: like the hexagonal and lozenge-shaped panels they are the object of a continuing programme of restoration, and it may be that one or other of them is temporarily not on display.

The statues from the Campanile

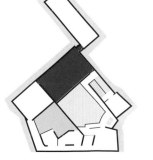

Along the entrance wall we see the four statues set up in 1343 on the west side, that is to say the main side, as it faces the same way as the façade of the Cathedral. These sculptures, by Andrea Pisano, remained in place until 1464, when they were moved to the north side to make room for the ones by Donatello. Rather than statues in the round these are very high reliefs, left unfinished at the back where they were concealed by the niches.

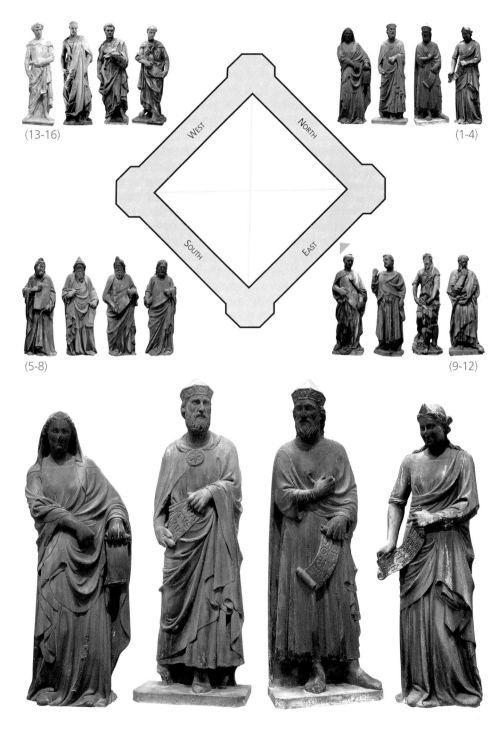

(13-16)

WEST

NORTH

(1-4)

SOUTH

EAST

(5-8)

(9-12)

On the previous page (p. 101), the arrangement of the statues on the four sides of the Campanile (after 1464) and, below, the sculptures by ANDREA PISANO, initially located on the west side and then moved to the north side in 1464, to make place for the ones by Donatello and Nanni di Bartolo (→ pp. 105-107): the *Tiburtine Sibyl*, *King David* (opposite, left, a detail; on the scroll we read the opening of Psalm I, "Blessed is the man who"), *King Solomon* (on the scroll, "Love Justice") and the *Erythraean Sibyl*. Kreytenberg believes that only the *Solomon* was by Andrea; the other three sculptures, "very similar to the work of Andrea Pisano, without however fully reaching his quality", are to be ascribed to his son Nino. Below, the *Prophets* which adorned the south side. The first from the left, probably *Moses* (he holds two large tablets in his hand), has been attributed to MASO DI BANCO because it closely resembles the figure of Pope St Sylvester painted by the artist in the Bardi di Vernio Chapel in the church of Santa Croce. Opposite, right, the third *Prophet*.

From left to right we have the TIBURTINE SIBYL and then – after the Della Robbia reliefs, which we shall come to in a moment – DAVID, SOLOMON and the ERYTHRAEAN SIBYL. These subjects allude to prophecies of the Redemption taken from the Old Testament and from pagan antiquity; the two sibyls were in addition believed by medieval Florentines to have uttered obscure prophecies about the birth of Florence. With the fluid rhythm of the drapery and the careful treatment of the surfaces, the four statues are still gothic in feeling.   1-4

A greater sense of volume and a more classical style characterise the four PROPHETS on the long wall opposite, which at one time stood in the niches on the south side. The differences in style from the earlier statues led scholars to ascribe them to Andrea Pisano's last period (after 1348); more recently the first figure on the left – presumably a MOSES – has been attributed to Maso di Banco, the second to Andrea and Nino Pisano, the third to the Master of the Scaffolding and the fourth also to Maso. They are now thought to date from between 1334 and 1341.   5-8   5

On the wall to the right of the entrance are four statues from the east side of the Campanile. Sculpted between 1408 and 1421, they represent PROPHETS and PATRIARCHS with profound realism and massive intensity. The only images whose subject is certain is the group show-   9-12

Below, the sculptures from the east side of the Campanile: the *Beardless Prophet*, by DONATELLO; a *Prophet* attributed to NANNI DI BARTOLO KNOWN AS ROSSO; the group of *Abraham and Isaac*, by DONATELLO and NANNI DI BARTOLO; the *Bearded Prophet*, by DONATELLO. The Opera commissioned the *Abraham and Isaac* from the two artists on 10 March 1421: only Nanni was present at the stipulation of the contract, and he accepted on behalf of his associate. To avoid losing commissions on account of the temporary absence of a partner was one of the main advantages of this type of collaboration between artists, which Donatello was to repeat with Michelozzo. The choice of subject was certainly not new: in 1401 the *Sacrifice of Isaac* had been set as the subject for the famous competition for the Baptistery's North door. Of the trial reliefs only those by FILIPPO BRUNELLESCHI and by the winner LORENZO GHIBERTI survive, now in the Bargello (above).

ing Abraham about to sacrifice his son Isaac. From the left we have: the so-called BEARDLESS PROPHET by Donatello, traditionally taken to be a portrait of his long-time friend Filippo Brunelleschi; the BEARDED PROPHET, which some have ascribed to Nanni di Bartolo known as Rosso, Donatello's assistant; the ABRAHAM AND ISAAC, by Donatello and Nanni di Bartolo; and finally a second BEARDED PROPHET, also known as *Il Penserioso* or 'the Thoughtful One', by Donatello.

The statues of the last group were originally located on the north side of the Campanile. In 1464 they were moved to the west side – in place of "four very clumsy figures" (Andrea Pisano's *Kings* and *Sibyls*) – so that "their beauties could be seen": from this time date some of the inscriptions at the base of the statues, not always pertinent ones.

Right, the *Prophet* identified by some as St John the Baptist and the *Abdias* by NANNI DI BARTOLO, whose scroll reads "Nanni il Rosso sculpted me, the prophet Abdias". There is no doubt as to the paternity of the *Habacuc*, which Vasari says is a portrait of Giovanni di Barduccio Chierichini, a rich self-made Florentine. It seems that DONATELLO was accustomed to swear by the statue and to invite it to speak: anecdotes undoubtedly motivated by the masterpiece's astonishing realism. With the first 22 florins he received from the Opera del Duomo, the artist paid off his tax arrears.

Between 1420 and 1435 the last four statues were made for the Campanile. The final side to be decorated should have been the north side, but it was decided to move Andrea Pisano's statues there and to replace them on the west side with the new ones. They now stand against the wall with the door leading into the Room of the Panels (and as usual we proceed from left to right).

The first PROPHET (ca. 1425) holds a scroll with the words 13
ECCE AGNUS DEI ("Behold the Lamb of God"), leading some scholars to identify him as *St John the Baptist*. The signature "Donatello" on the base is very obviously later than the date of the statue, which is in fact perhaps by Nanni di Bartolo.

Next to it is HABACUC, also known as *Lo Zuccone* or 14
'Pumpkin-head' (1423-1435), Donatello's masterpiece. The emaciated, ascetic form of the prophet is wrapped in a long tunic, falling from the left shoulder, the deep folds of which are expressive of inner torment. The half-open mouth seems about to utter terrible prophecies. According to popular tradition Donatello used as his model for the statue of Habacuc an enemy of the Medici family, Giovanni Chiericini.

In addition to Habacuc (opposite), the eighth of the twelve Minor Prophets of the Old Testament, DONATELLO sculpted a *Jeremias* (below, right). This austere prophet, with his harsh rebukes and insistent calls to penitence, lived in a dramatic period in the history of Israel. The Babylonians, having overrun the Assyrian empire, captured Jerusalem in 586 BC and deported a large part of the population to Babylon: on this occasion Jeremias invited the Hebrews to respect the will of God and to submit to the "Babylonian yoke". So savagely did he rail against man's wickedness that he was several times arrested. Like the *Habacuc*, the *Jeremias* was believed to be a real portrait, this time the model being Francesco Soderini, a friend of the sculptor.

JEREMIAS (1427-1435) is another of Donatello's works 15 characterised by profound psychological penetration. The head of the prophet, turned to the left, is expressive of intense bitterness, with its down-turned mouth and tension in the muscles of the neck. Unlike the *Habacuc*, the drapery shows considerable movement: there are two great folds, an upper one which leaves the breast partially uncovered, and a lower one which accentuates the movement of the left leg. This statue, too, was popularly believed to portray an enemy of the Medici, Francesco Soderini, whose descendant Piero became Gonfalonier of the Florentine Republic, and was a friend of Niccolò Machiavelli.

ABDIAS (ca. 1422) is by Nanni di Bartolo, a sculptor who 16 was influenced by Donatello but did not lack originality, as can be seen from his sinuous treatment of line.

Today we are apt to ascribe intrinsic value to anything that qualifies as antique (or even simply old). It has not always been thus: "in the past it was common practice to replace antiques with new artistic creations, whenever they seemed worn out or no longer corresponded to the aesthetic criteria of the age" (Giusti). Distinguished victims of this custom were the groups of Tino di Camaino (→ pp. 16-20) and the statues of the old façade (→ pp. 22-42). In 1688 the Cantorie by LUCA DELLA ROBBIA (above) and DONATELLO (opposite) suffered the same fate: considered to be outdated and too small, they were removed and replaced by large wooden structures (which in turn were replaced in the 19th century by stone ones). After much discussion as to whether the cantorie should be reassembled in the Cathedral or in the Bargello, they were remounted by the Opera in its own headquarters, and the Opera del Duomo Museum created around the two masterpieces.

The Cantorie

We come now to the two Cantorie, remembering that the Museum of the Opera was created to house, and developed around, these great masterpieces of the Florentine Renaissance.

A *cantoria* is an open box or singing-gallery for the choristers who sang the liturgical chants. Located near the organ, or in this case directly beneath it, it has an extremely simple structure: two or more consoles attached to the wall support a floor surrounded by a parapet. To the purely functional role was added a decorative one, and it was not by chance that these magnificent examples were commissioned from great artists like Luca della Robbia and Donatello.

The scheme, put into effect immediately after the construction of the dome, was devised by Filippo Brunelleschi himself. The singing-gallery to be placed above the door of the Sacristy of the Masses, also known as the New Sacristy, was to be by Luca, who had the easier task as that side is better lit. The young but already acclaimed sculptor began work in 1431, one year before Matteo da Prato began building the two organs, and completed it in 1438. Donatello worked for about the same length of time

(from 1433 to 1439) on his singing-gallery, which was to go above the door of the Old or Canons' Sacristy; his task, however, was much more difficult, because the right side is shadier.

For two and a half centuries the two cantorie remained in position, to universal admiration, until in 1688 the crown prince Ferdinando, son of the Grand Duke Cosimo III, married Violante of Bavaria. Their wedding was celebrated in the Cathedral with unheard-of splendour: the Grand Ducal architects actually covered the entire façade with bricks, which were then plastered and painted with fictive architecture. The preparations also affected the interior, and as the cantorie were considered too small as well as outdated in style, they were relegated to the deposits of the Opera: only the consoles and the floors remained, which served as bases for two enormous intarsiated cantorie in typical baroque style. In the 1840s the architect Gaetano Baccani built the present stone structures, so that the remaining original portions went to join those removed in the 17th century. With the first opening of the Museum (1887) the two cantorie were reassembled, and the places of a few missing portions were filled by modern replacements.

The Cantoria of Luca della Robbia

We begin with the CANTORIA by Luca della Robbia, which is on the entrance wall. Above, we see a complete reconstruction, with casts replacing the original sculptures; below, we can admire the originals. Of the ten reliefs, six were mounted on the parapet and four in the spaces between the five consoles. According to Vasari, Luca's Cantoria was surmounted by two bronze angels, now lost.

The subject is Psalm 150, attributed to King David. The Latin verses are distributed in three lines: the upper one is carved on the cornice, the second on the base of the parapet and the third on the base of the consoles. The text on the cornice reads: "Praise ye the Lord in his holy places: praise ye him in the firmament of his power. Praise ye him for his mighty acts: praise ye him according to the multitude of his greatness"; on the base of the parapet: "Praise him with sound of trumpet, praise him with psaltery and harp. Praise him with timbrel…"; on the base of the consoles: "…and choir: praise him with strings and organs. Praise him on high sounding cymbals: praise him on cymbals of joy: let every spirit praise the Lord".

17

In preparation for the consecration of the Cathedral, to be dedicated to the Virgin and to the city, "the Opera hurried up the internal and external decoration, at least in the more essential areas" (Settesoldi). The Operai had decided to have two cantorie made, to place over the doors of the sacristies in the Cathedral: the Canons' Sacristy and the Sacristy of the Masses (the latter was intended to receive the Cathedral's new organ, ordered from Matteo da Prato in 1432). The name of Luca della Robbia appears for the first time in connection with the Cantoria for the Sacristy of the Masses in a document of 1431; it is not impossible, however, that the project was begun a few years earlier, especially as three years previously the Arte della Lana had frozen all the finances on account of the war with Milan. Luca began with the side panels (opposite, above, the left one), completing two reliefs per year. The later panels, judged to be better and therefore paid for at a higher rate, show the influence of the dancing putti on Donatello's pulpit for Prato Cathedral (⟶ p. 115), a work whose great impact on artists and public is attested by a letter written in 1434 by the same Matteo da Prato. For the Cantoria, finished in 1438, Luca received a total of 872 florins. The scenes represented in the panels were possibly suggested by Matteo da Prato himself and illustrate the well-known verses of Psalm CL, *Laudate Dominum*, which has been set to music by numerous composers (there is a famous setting for solo voice by Claudio Monteverdi). The panels shown at right, the first (above) and third (below) of the parapet, illustrate the verses in which the people are invited to praise the Lord with the sound of trumpet (*in sono tubae*) and harp (*in cythara*). According to Vasari, Luca also made two figures of gilded bronze, perhaps the two *Candle-bearing Angels* now in the Musée Jacquemart-André, Paris.

Acknowledged as "the greatest and purest classicist of the 15th century" (De Marchi), LUCA DELLA ROBBIA developed a sculptural style of great formal rigour, enriched with stupendous rhythmical modulations; the naturalness and composedness of his works make him the direct heir of Nanni di Banco (→ p. 34). Vasari tells us that Luca "was sent by his father to learn the art of goldsmithery with Leonardo di ser Giovanni", from whom he learned "to draw and to work in wax". In those days it was normal to become an artist by training with a goldsmith: Filippo Brunelleschi's father, too, "made him learn the abacus and writing, and then sent him to a goldsmith, so that he could learn to draw". According to Gentilini, this apprenticeship of Luca's helps to explain the technical and formal peculiarities of his later production: in Vasari's words, his proverbial "diligence" in "polishing and finishing" the marble, his great skill in modelling wax and clay, his "very good and graceful drawing". Vasari says that Luca della Robbia made his Cantoria "finishing everything much more neatly than Donato himself did": the fluid, classical elegance of Luca was in the end more appreciated than the unquiet art of Donatello, even by Brunelleschi, who for many years had been Donatello's great friend. After his early work in marble Luca applied himself for the most part to terracotta, perfecting his special glazing technique and giving rise to an almost industrial production, which was to be continued by his descendants for generations and achieved enormous popularity – especially in 19th-century England.

Right: the second (above) and fourth (below) panels of the lower series, separated by console, show players of the organ, harp, lute and cymbals; opposite, the first panel of the lower series (above, with a dancing choir) and the side panel on the right (below).

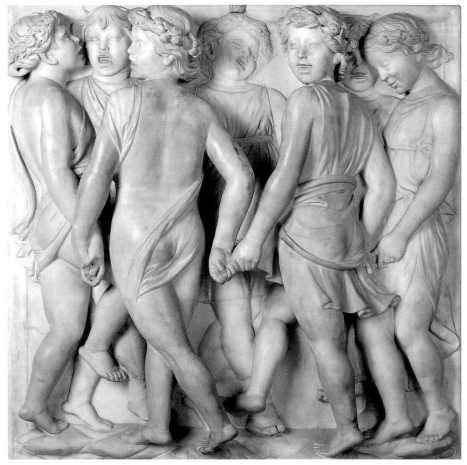

To illustrate the scriptural text the artist shows groups of children singing, playing instruments and dancing. The two lateral reliefs on the parapet show singers from books and scrolls; the four frontal ones show children playing the trumpet, psaltery, cithara and drum; the four between the consoles show others dancing, and playing the organ, harp, lute, drum, tambourine and cymbals. The accuracy of representation is not restricted to compositional elements: Luca descends to particulars, analysing the attitudes and feelings of the individual musicians. The sculptures, in high relief, stand out on the smooth parapet, divided by ten paired pilaster-strips. The overall effect is one of classical grace and composure, typical of the full renaissance style; the artist's technical mastery is all the more astonishing when we recall that this is his very first known work.

The Cantoria for the Sacristy of the Canons was commissioned from DONATELLO on his return from Rome: the contract of 14 November 1433 established a price of 40 florins per piece if it turned out as well as Luca's, "and should it be more perfect he can have 50 florins per piece". As he had already done with the *St John the Evangelist*, Donatello sculpted the Cantoria in a chapel inside the Cathedral, assisted by workmen provided by the Opera. In 1438 the work was described in the documents as almost ready (*prope finitum*); there remained only a few minor details, such as the second head beside the central console, for which the sculptor received 300 *libbre* (about 30 kilograms) of bronze. In 1446 the value of the work was assessed by experts at 886 florins, but the Operai laid down that Donatello could collect what was still owing to him (he had already received several payments on account) from Cosimo de' Medici's bank only six months after he had cast in bronze the doors of that same Canons' Sacristy: he had been awarded the commission in 1437, but these bronze doors were never made.

The Cantoria of Donatello

The CANTORIA on the opposite wall is very different. As we have said, Donatello had to deal with a not inconsiderable obstacle, the fact that the side where his Cantoria was to go is in permanent shadow. He had to make the maximum use of what light there was, and to devise evocative effects.

To achieve his aim the master drew inspiration from the rich decoration of Arnolfo's façade, designing a structure of polychrome marbles and interspersing it with mosaic. Five consoles support a not very deep loggia consisting of five pairs of columns decorated with mosaic; against the background of the portico, also covered in mosaic, a continuous relief shows a dance of putti. In the two outer spaces between the consoles are pairs of putti; from the inner ones protrude two bronze heads, originally gilded. Strangely identical, the bronzes derive from an unknown classical model and have perhaps a symbolical significance which eludes us.

The theme of the Cantoria, suggested by the head of the Opera Neri Capponi, finds many parallels in the art of antiquity, but Donatello treats it in an entirely original and anti-classical fashion. The agitated and almost frenzied rhythm of his composition, inscrted into an architectural framework composed of disparate elements and materials, sets up an opposition with the work of Luca. The treatment of the material is also utterly different: whereas the young Della Robbia polishes his figures and exactly

18

DONATELLO's Cantoria is in many respects an experimental work, first of all because of the deliberately rough but highly effective technique employed by the artist, who "made the figures in rough, which when seen from the ground seem truly to live and to move" (Vasari); the Anonimo Magliabechiano made a similar observation ("the figures are all roughed out and unfinished and from the ground seem by no means the less"). Having set aside the sobriety and severity of his youthful works, Donatello continues here the search begun in 1428 with the pulpit of Prato Cathedral, which he made with the assistance of Michelozzo and Pagno di Lapo: the joyful vitality of the genii on the pulpit appears even more dynamic and accentuated in the putti on the Cantoria, hurtling in a dance which the architecture of the loggia and the impalpable background seem to exalt rather than restrain. Another unusual element in the decoration is the use of gilded and multi-coloured tesserae. When it was still not known that Arnolfo di Cambio had made extensive use of mosaic on the cathedral façade, some scholars explained its presence on the Cantoria with the influence of early-Christian art, and deduced that Donatello was taking an anti-classical position; we now know that in reality he had examples of mosaic and intarsia in front of his eyes. Right, the *Madonna and Child* attributed to PAGNO DI LAPO PORTIGIANI. Other suggestions have been Agostino di Duccio (Janson) and Antonio Rossellino (Brunetti).

defines their contours, anticipating in some way his future work in glazed terracotta, Donatello treats his surfaces roughly and approximately, in a fashion which the genius of Michelangelo would later develop into his celebrated *non finito*.

It would be fascinating to know whether and to what extent the two artists came to an agreement about their different approaches to the work assigned to them. The fact is that on this occasion two great artists together produced two different views of life, two antithetical modes of conceiving the world: the 'Apollonian' one of Luca, and the 'Dionysian' one of Donatello.

The Room of the Silver Altar contains examples of the so-called 'minor' arts (goldsmiths' work, textiles, miniatures). From the mid-14th century onwards these arts, the focus of much experimentation, received a decisive impulse from the requirement for adequate furnishings in the Cathedral and Baptistery; in the 15th century there would be remarkable technical advances, contributing to the development of many new ideas.

On the right wall of the Room of the Cantorie a door leads into a small circular space; on the right is a marble bas-relief of the MADONNA AND CHILD. *Although not startlingly origi-* 19 *nal, this typical renaissance sculpture, which has been at the Opera since the 17th century, stirs our admiration with the measured elegance of its figures and with the air of sweet and subtle melancholy pervading it. In the 16th century it was attributed to Pagno di Lapo Portigiani by Giorgio Vasari, although recently the name of the better known Antonio Rossellino has been proposed.*
We now come to one of the most interesting rooms in the Museum, the Room of the Silver Altar, so called from a precious piece of furnishing from the Baptistery of San Giovanni, moved here in 1891.

13. The Room of the Silver Altar

On the wall to the right of the entrance is a large polychrome wooden CRUCIFIX from the Baptistery. This work, 1 rich in pathos and accurate in its rendering of anatomy, is attributed to Giovanni di Balduccio and may be dated to around 1330. The Christ has moveable arms, so that it could be used to enact the Deposition from the Cross during the Holy Week ceremonies.

Right, polychrome wooden *Crucifix* (ca. 1330) attributed to GIOVANNI DI BALDUCCIO. It comes from the Baptistery, where it remained from 1333 to 1912. The altar where it stood, beside the Door of Paradise, was rearranged many times over the centuries: the final version, dating from 1741, was dismantled in the early 20th century. The arms of Christ, originally moveable but later fixed close to the body, have been returned to their original position by the restorers, who also revealed the presence of a wooden insert on the face – upper lip, teeth and part of the moustache – presumably due to a *pentimento* on the part of the artist. Restoration has also revealed the original colours: the highly effective red of the blood was obtained by the use of pure cinnabar. This sculpture was the object of intense devotion, especially as it was held to be "made from the wood of the elm which burst into flower on being touched by the bier carrying the body of St Zenobius" (Del Migliore; → p. 44-45). It is undoubtedly one of the highest achievements of early 14th-century Italian sculpture; among the names which have been proposed for its author – in addition to the one offered here – are those of Andrea and Giovanni Pisano (later 13th century).

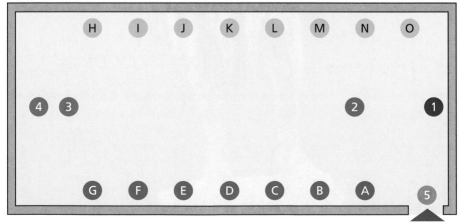

It has been observed that not until full 16th-century Mannerism could anyone hope to understand and appreciate DONATELLO's late works. Having returned to Florence (1454) after a sojourn in Padua, the old sculptor found a city in which the ideals of classicising elegance prevailed, and yet he went his own way; in other words he continued to experiment, and to develop his preferred themes: "plurality of viewpoints, the unfleshing of forms, the ever more certain conquest of space achieved by the rotation of figures" (Bertelà). It was in this period that – in addition to two *St John the Baptists*, one in bronze (Siena) and the other in wood (Venice) – Donatello sculpted a *Magdalene* "consumed by fasting and abstinence" (Vasari) in white poplar wood. The date of another wooden *Magdalene* (now in the Collegiata Museum, Empoli) made in the workshop of Neri di Bicci and clearly inspired by Donatello's allows us to date the latter to around 1455. A masterpiece of veristic naturalism, this spectral figure (Rosenauer calls it a "living mummy") represents the crisis and the rejection of that classicism of which Donatello as a young man had been the principal exponent. The presence of the statue in the Baptistery is attested in 1500 by a payment made by the Arte di Calimala to the goldsmith Jacopo Sogliani for "the diadem made for the figure and image of St Mary Magdalene"; but it seems that the statue was already in San Giovanni in 1494, when the French king Charles VIII, encamped at the gates of Florence with his army, offered enormous sums of money for it (Del Migliore). Later the statue was moved several times, so that it is possible that it never was intended for a specific location. Very badly damaged by the 1966 flood, it was moved to the Museum in 1972 after a lengthy restoration which recovered fillets of gold in the hair – the pale reflection of a beauty disfigured by self-mortification.

The Magdalene of Donatello

Near the door, in the centre, stands Donatello's intense masterpiece, the MAGDALENE (1453-1455), sculpted for the Baptistery. As he had done many years earlier when working on the Cantoria, the aged master chose the material with a view to the effects which lighting would confer on his work. Wood is difficult to work in that unlike marble or stone it does not allow soft shading or passages of gradation: for this reason wooden sculpture, so common in the schematic spiritualised art of the Middle Ages, became sporadic in the Renaissance. But Donatello, the renaissance artist par excellence, chose it deliberately because he wanted to treat an unusual and pathetic subject, one susceptible of dramatic contrasts: the theme of ascesis through mortification of the flesh. The emaciated Magdalene, with her hollow-eyed, ravaged face, wasted frame, prominent veins and tendons, and long shaggy hair, holds her hands not quite touching in prayer, but slightly apart, in a gesture of stupor at the miracle by which Jesus freed her from "seven devils" (Mark 16:9; Luke 8:2), and at the unfathomable mystery of the Resurrection. The half-parted lips – allowing us to glimpse the teeth – and the astonished gaze seem absorbed by the mystery of salvation: in its compressed and anguished immobility the entire image pulses with an inexpressible sense of pity.

The sculptor painted his statue and finished it with tow (for the hair) and plaster (for certain details). As well as reinforcing the work's naturalistic effect, the choice of these humble materials is in itself an anti-classical gesture which symbolises the profound unease of Donatello's last period: an unease which acted as a spur, producing very different results, to both Leonardo and Michelangelo.

The Silver Altar of St John the Baptist

At the far end of the room some steps lead up to the SILVER ALTAR OF ST JOHN THE BAPTIST. This rich and elaborate work is enclosed within a special container which preserves it in nitrogen, at the correct humidity and temperature; it too will shortly be restored, because the oxidisation of the silver has badly affected the overlying gilding. Begun in 1367 as an altar-dossal, it was used until the end of the 14th century to decorate the front of the high altar in the Baptistery; it was then attached to a mobile altar set up in the centre of the building, upon which twice a year – on 13 January, feast of the Baptism of Christ, and on 24 June, feast of the Nativity of St John the Baptist – the church's Treasure

Dante called Florence the "city which changed into the Baptist its first patron", i.e. the god Mars. Exactly when this 'change' took place, that is to say when the cult of St John was introduced to the city, is uncertain: some attribute it to Theodolinda, wife of the Longobard Agilulf, who ordered a church dedicated to him (ca. 625); others propose a later date (down to the 11th century). The official feast day of the city's patron fell, and still falls, on 24 June, but the celebrations lasted for many days. From the later 16th century the silver altar (or dossal) was set up on the centre of the Baptistery, piled with all the relics and reliquaries belonging to the Arte di Calimala, which held the patronage of the building. Another feast when the so-called Treasure of San Giovanni was shown to the people was 13 January, the Octave of the Epiphany, when the Baptism of Christ was commemorated: on 13 January 1413 the schismatic antipope John XXIII (Baldassarre Coscia, → p. 131) had granted a plenary indulgence, later confirmed by Martin V and Eugenius IV. Every 6 November another exposition of the Treasure celebrated the dedication of the Baptistery by Pope Nicholas II in the 11th century (6 November 1059).

was displayed for the admiration of the faithful. The central aedicule was added in 1441, and the statuette of the BAPTIST was placed inside it eleven years later. In 1477 it was decided to transform the dossal into a free-standing altar, providing it with two flanks ornamented with reliefs; they were completed in 1483, which is when the wooden cornices, above and below, seem also to have been added.

The altar was commissioned by the Calimala Guild, who seem to have spared no expense: indeed, it required almost 400 kilograms of silver. Enriched with enamels and gilding, it has an overall architectural structure of late gothic design: a moulded gilded wooden base supports six polygonal piers, divided into two by horizontal cornices, and decorated with niches containing cast statuettes of saints. Along the top runs a frieze consisting of a continuous row of niches, each one containing a statuette. Above the frieze is an elaborate cornice of carved and gilded wood. Between the base of the piers and the frieze are twelve reliefs (eight frontal and four lateral panels) with scenes from the life of the Baptist. The centre is occupied by the aedicule with the statue of the Saint.

The wooden cornice is plausibly attributed to the workshop of Giuliano da Maiano. The first phase of work on the dossal involved the silversmiths Leonardo di ser Giovanni, Betto di Geri, Cristofano di Paolo and Michele di Monte, who completed the frontal by the end of the 14th century. We are not able to identify the individual contributions of these silversmiths, who were all heavily influenced by Andrea Orcagna; but we do know that the aedicule was made in Ghiberti's workshop, and that the stat-

In the 1360s the Arte di Calimala decided to dismantle the 13th-century dossal on the high altar of the Baptistery and to commission another and more magnificent one. The new dossal required more than a hundred years' work (from 1366, as is recorded in the inscription at the base of the altar, to ca. 1483) and involved the greatest artists of several generations: from Leonardo di ser Giovanni, who may have designed the reliefs, to Michele di Monte and Cristofano di Paolo; from Tommaso Ghiberti and Matteo di Giovanni, who from 1445 to 1452 worked on the central niche (where Michelozzo's *Baptist* was inserted), to Bernardo Cennini, Antonio del Pollaiolo, Andrea del Verrocchio and Antonio di Salvi (1477-1483: the commission was to have gone to the winner of a competition, but in fact the reliefs were divided between the participants). So the silver altar represents a kind of synthesis of the main tendencies in Florentine silversmithery and sculpture from the gothic age until the full-blown Renaissance (Paolucci). It is in good state of conservation, even if over the centuries small parts (enamels, heads, etc.) became detached, and thirteen statuettes have been lost or stolen. Continual remounting and rearranging have several times altered the sequence of the reliefs: the scenes showing the Saint baptising the people and the Saint before Herod, for example, have now exchanged places, as we can tell from old descriptions and early-20th-century photographs. During the expositions of the Treasure (of which we have a description by Piero Cennini, son of the silversmith Bernardo), the altar became the centre of the city (*umbilicus urbis*), the symbol of the piety (and of the power) of the Republic (Paolucci). Above, *Annunciation to Zacharias and Visitation*, by BERNARDO CENNINI: the silversmith was also an engraver and a printer. Below, the *Banquet of Herod* by ANTONIO DI SALVI SALVUCCI and FRANCESCO DI GIOVANNI.

BERNARDO CENNINI, ANNUNCIATION TO ZACHARIAS AND VISITATION	JESUS VISITING THE BAPTIST IN THE WILDERNESS	BAPTISM OF CHRIST	THE BAPTIST BEFORE HEROD	CHRIST RECEIVES THE MESSENGERS FROM THE BAPTIST	ANTONIO DI SALVI SALVUCCI, BANQUET OF HEROD
ANTONIO DEL POLLAIOLO, BIRTH OF THE BAPTIST	ST JOHN SETTING OUT INTO THE WILDERNESS	ST JOHN PREACHING TO THE MULTITUDE	ST JOHN BAPTISING THE PEOPLE	THE BAPTIST VISITED BY HIS DISCIPLES IN PRISON	ANDREA DEL VERROCCHIO, BEHEADING OF THE BAPTIST

Top, the iconographic scheme of the silver dossal; above, the statue of *St John the Baptist* by MICHELOZZO. Opposite, the silver cross which the Arte di Calimala commissioned in 1457 from ANTONIO DEL POLLAIOLO (→ pp. 144-147), BETTO DI FRANCESCO BETTI and MILIANO DI DOMENICO DEI to contain a relic of the True Cross traditionally believed to have been donated to the city by the emperor Charlemagne. Rivalry between guilds was a fact of Florentine life, and the Calimala's actions seems to have been prompted by a desire not to be outdone by the 'rival' Arte della Lana, which two years earlier had acquired by the Greek Marco Chestialselim its own relic of the True Cross (later placed inside the Gold Cross, → pp. 62-63).

ue of St John, sculpted in a deliberately archaic style, is by Michelozzo di Bartolomeo. The authors of the reliefs on the flanks are also known.

Let us look at the reliefs in narrative order.

On the left flank: above, *Zacharias and the Angel*, and the *Visitation*, by Bernardo Cennini; below, the *Birth of the Baptist*, by Antonio del Pollaiolo.

On the left side of the frontal: bottom left, *St John setting out into the wilderness*; bottom right, *St John preaching to the multitude*; top left, *Jesus visiting the Baptist in the wilderness*; top right, *the Baptism of Christ*.

On the right side of the frontal: top left, *The Baptist before Herod*; top right, *Christ receives the messengers from the Baptist*; bottom left, *St John baptising the people*; bottom right, *The Baptist visited by his disciples in prison*.

On the right flank: below, the *Beheading of the Baptist*, by Andrea del Verrocchio; above, the *Banquet of Herod*, by Antonio di Salvi Salvucci.

The Silver Cross

Above the dossal stands a great silver CROSS decorated 4 with enamels. The documentation on this work is fairly full, or seems so at first sight. It was commissioned by the Calimala for the Baptistery, and made between 1457 and 1459 by three artists from the Florentine area: Betto di Francesco Betti worked on the upper portion, while the lower was completed by Antonio del Pollaiolo and Miliano di Domenico Dei. Some critics, however, have doubts about the authorship of the Christ and the two statuettes on the arm: the names of both Bernardo Cennini and Luca della Robbia have been proposed. There is also discussion about the object's function. Originally it was perhaps intended as a reliquary or ostensorium: the Calimala had for centuries owned a fragment of the True Cross, which according to legend had been presented to Florence by Charlemagne. Then, in 1455 the Arte della Lana or Wool

The silver Cross was delivered in 1459; however, the reference in a document to the fact that Pollaiolo was working on it in 1468 led Luisa Becherucci to suppose that its execution had taken place in two distinct phases: the base would be a work of Pollaiolo's maturity, when the artist had already enriched his personal cultural baggage by the 'discovery' of Donatello. The Cross bears on the front the figure of the Crucifix sculpted in the round (right), of uncertain attribution. The hexagonal *tempietto* supporting the Cross is inspired by the lantern designed by Brunelleschi for the dome of Santa Maria del Fiore: similar derivations are encountered in many reliquaries and liturgical objects of the later 15th century (Liscia Bemporad). The iconographic scheme is subdivided into two cycles: the sacrifice of Christ, on the Cross itself, and the figure of the Baptist (who announces the coming of the Messias and of the Kingdom of the Redemption), on the stele and the base. Antonio di Jacopo Benci and his brother Piero were called 'del Pollaiolo' after the profession of their father, who had a poultry shop in the Old Market. The two brothers often collaborated and it is often difficult to distinguish their contributions. Their varied production (paintings, sculptures, goldsmith's work), exercised considerable influence over the development of Florentine art. Having worked for many years in Florence, where their workshop became one of the most important and esteemed in the city, the two brothers moved to Rome in 1484. Antonio, an outstanding designer of human figures in motion, was one of the first artists to practise anatomical dissection to study the human body, anticipating the great Leonardo da Vinci. The other two silversmiths who worked on the Cross, MILIANO DEI and BETTO BETTI, belonged to an older generation than Antonio's. Opposite, the back of the Cross (upper portion).

Guild, which held the patronage of the Cathedral, acquired a similar relic of its own: a certain amount of rivalry seems to have grown up between the two corporations, which might have induced the Calimala to have its fragment enclosed within a reliquary of high artistic value. Towards the end of the century the piece lost its function as a reliquary and received the additions of the Crucified Christ and the lateral statuettes.

On the front, at the extremities of the arms, there are four enamels: at the top God the Father, on the right the Virgin, on the left St John the Apostle, and at the bottom the Magdalene. At the intersection, behind the head of Christ, is the Pelican in her piety, the symbol of sacrifice; half-way down the lower arm is the portrait of a Saint. On the back, at the extremities of the arms there are the Four Evangelists; at the intersection, the *Agnus Dei* surrounded by Prophets; half-way down the lower arm, St John the Baptist setting out for the wilderness.

The Cross rests on a Calvary in relief, with a skull surrounded by an idealised representation of Jerusalem. Below there are two roundels, decorated with Saints on one side and an Annunciation on the other. From them rise two arms supporting the statuettes of the Virgin and St John. On the node there are representations of the Baptist on both the back and the front: he is shown seated within a *tempietto*, flanked by angels. On the polylobed foot there are reliefs showing the Baptism of Christ, the Doctors of the Church, Moses, the Theological Virtues, Temperance, two Angels and coats of arms of the Calimala (an eagle grasping in its talons a bale of cloth). At the sides, a pair of harpies support two Angels cast in the round.

The glass cases on the left wall

The glass cases which cover the long walls of the room contain a series of precious liturgical objects. We proceed as usual from left to right, beginning at the entrance door; for convenience we indicate the glass cases by letters of the alphabet.

Case A. Religious ceremonies are accompanied by singing and readings. Both texts and music were collected in large parchment volumes, which on account of their bulk were placed on lecterns known as *badaloni*: we saw a fine example of one in the Room of the Paintings (→ p. 57). The Cathedral and the Baptistery possessed a large collection of these volumes – antiphonaries, missals, graduals and evangeliaria – all beautifully copied and illuminated in the late 15th and early 16th century. During the 1966 flood many of the fifty-eight existing codices were unfortunately submerged in water, some of them being irreparably damaged. The work of restoration, requiring very high levels of skill and considerable time, has recovered a number of examples completely, but will not be entirely finished for several more years.

The visitor should be warned that the codex currently displayed in the upper part of the case may be replaced by another one, or else the page may be turned: this is because light, whether natural or artificial, tends to make the colours fade.

At the time of writing, number 11 is on display: an Antiphonary of 126 leaves, containing the *Proprium de tempore* from the Epiphany to the Saturday before Septuagesima, made between 1513 and 1526, and illustrated with splendid initial letters by the mosaicist, painter and miniaturist Monte di Giovanni. The codex is currently open at leaves 4 and 5. The verso of leaf 4 shows the initial H, illustrating the *Baptism of Christ*. On the left are three kneeling angels and two prelates, one of whom seems to be Pope Leo X (Giovanni de' Medici, 1475-1521, pope from 1513). In the background, a city on the banks of the river Jordan; above, God the Father and the dove of the Holy Spirit. In the decorative outer margin we recognise the *Agnus Dei*, symbol, as we know, of both the Arte della Lana and the Opera del Duomo. Below, there is an allegorical scene: a lioness, two lions and a bear are shut in a cage and playing with five golden balls (the charges on the Medici coat of arms); from two laurel bushes, one of which is cut down (alluding to Lorenzo the Magnificent's

A.1

The Opera, which had begun to commission precious volumes for the Cathedral in the second half of the 15th century, embarked on an intense new campaign of codex production at the beginning of the following century. By the end of this undertaking, in which master miniaturists such as Frate Eustachio or brothers Gherardo and Monte di Giovanni took part, "Santa Maria del Fiore could finally boast a most precious cycle of liturgical books, not inferior either in number or in value to those of any other church" (Tacconi). In a miniature (right) from an antiphonary now in the Archive of the Opera (Cod. E n. 24 fol. 50r), Frate Eustachio, a Dominican friar from San Marco, shows *Esau setting off to hunt* and taking leave of his father Isaac in the courtyard, while upstairs Rachel and Jacob prepare to deceive the old man with the skins of goats. Below, the singular *ex-voto* of Anichino Corsi.

heraldic device of a *semper virens* stump, the branch of an evergreen tree), hang the arms of the People and of the city of Florence.

In the lower part of the case there is an object from the Treasure of San Giovanni, which as we have seen was displayed on the silver altar on the occasion of certain civic and religious feasts.

It is the EX-VOTO OF ANICHINO CORSI (1447), the work of A.2 the Florentine goldsmith Rinaldo di Giovanni di Ghino: an embossed parcel-gilt shaft supports a beautiful branch of red coral.

Anichino is a typical medieval Tuscan name – it occurs in Boccaccio (*Decameron* VII, 7), and is probably a corruption of the German patronym Johann Joachim – but all we know of this one is what we learn from the Latin inscription on the node of the shaft: that he fought against the Moors, and obtained the coral as booty in war. This was probably a raid against Saracen pirates, because the eighth and last Crusade was in 1270 (too early for the date of the object).

Above, a flood-damaged codex. Displayed on the ground floor since 1954, the collection was disastrously affected when the Arno burst its banks on 4 November 1966. The pages, soaked in mud, swelled and stuck to each other; miniatures, their glues and pigments dissolved, stuck to the opposite page or simply flaked off. Above, the Museum's great *badalone* on the eve of the flood: thanks to its height the three antiphonaries displayed on it suffered no damage. From two of them come two miniatures by FRATE EUSTACHIO (right): the *Plotting of the sons of Jacob* (above, Cod. E n. 24 fol. 93r), which will replace the page by Monte di Giovanni now displayed, and the *Annunciation* (below, Cod. M n. 25 fol. 70r). Frate Eustachio excels as a decorator and colourist: his elegant, quiet style (that of a "convent Renaissance") reveals the influence of Angelico. He seems to have had a prodigious memory, and to have been the unacknowledged source of many of the anecdotes related by Vasari in the first version of his *Lives*.

Many of the reliquaries preserved in the Museum are made up of elements of different provenance: this is the case of the reliquary of the arm of St Philip the Apostle (above, left). The base seems to have been made by Matteo di Lorenzo for the relics of the Grioni donation. The upper portion – the late-gothic *tempietto* with its statues of prophets – is by ANTONIO DI PIETRO DEL VAGLIENTE. The statue on the top has been attributed on account of its marked Donatello-like characteristics to Michelozzo, who in 1425 was a partner of the great sculptor. In the centre, the reliquary of the jaw-bone of St John the Baptist. The Pietro Cerluzi mentioned in the documents is not otherwise known; Diletta Corsini has proposed identifying him with Tommaso di Pietro Cambiuzi, who matriculated as a goldsmith in 1564. Right, the reliquary of the index-finger of St John the Baptist.

CASE B contains three reliquaries from the Baptistery. The first is the RELIQUARY OF THE ARM OF ST PHILIP THE APOSTLE AND OTHER RELICS (1425). The principal relic – bequeathed to the Baptistery in 1204 by Monaco de' Corbizzi (d. 1203), a Florentine cleric who became Patriarch of Jerusalem – reached Florence in a casket of gilded and enamelled silver, where it remained until 1422. In that year it was decided to commission a new reliquary, but only the upper portion is in fact the work of the goldsmith chosen, Antonio di Piero del Vagliente; the original base was lost during the tumultuous events of the Siege of Florence in 1529-1530, and two centuries later (1723) Bernardo Holzman replaced it with the present one. This is a hexagonal casket dated 1398 and probably the work of Matteo di Lorenzo; it originally contained relics of oriental provenance, as can be inferred from the Latin inscription, which mentions the Eastern emperor Manuel Palaeologus.

The second object on display is the RELIQUARY OF THE JAW-BONE OF ST JOHN THE BAPTIST, made of silver and partially gilded copper by Pietro Cerluzi (or Cambiuzi, as has recently been proposed). Perhaps it was for this relic, do-

B.1

B.2

nated in 1394 by the Venetian noblewoman Nicoletta Grioni (→ p. 139), that Matteo di Lorenzo made between 1397 and 1398 the "pedestal in gilded silver with six faces and six small lions" which now forms the base of the reliquary of St Philip (see above). The present container was made for Duke Cosimo in 1564: on a hexagonal, pyramidal foot a vase-shaped shaft, decorated with embossed leaves, supports the convex base of a hexagonal *tempietto*, the roof of which is surmounted by a cast statuette of the Baptist.

Next we have the RELIQUARY OF THE INDEX-FINGER OF ST JOHN THE BAPTIST (1698), by an anonymous master. It contains the most important of the Saint's relics preserved in Florence. According to tradition it belonged to Pope Urban V, who had been given it by the Patriarch of Constantinople in 1363; lost during the pontificate of Urban VI, it was recovered in 1386 by Baldassarre Coscia, at that time 'cleric of the chamber' to the pope. Coscia, who reigned as antipope ('John XXIII') for a time during the Great Schism (→ caption), ended his life in Florence, where he died in 1419. Wishing to be buried in the Baptistery he had bequeathed this and other relics to the Florentine Republic. In 1421 the Calimala, which held the patronage of the Baptistery, commissioned from Giovanni del Chiaro a reliquary "all covered with gold, silver and pearls", which the goldsmith completed two years later. Unfortunately the disastrous flood of 1557 seriously damaged this and other reliquaries of San Giovanni. The present one, of embossed silver, was made at the expense of the nobleman Francesco Maria Sergrifi. The triangular, pyramidal base supports a short stem bearing the arms of the donor; the aedicule containing the relic is decorated with three cherub's heads and is surmounted by a cast statuette of the *Agnus Dei* with cross and flag.

CASE C contains three more reliquaries. The first and third come from the Treasury of San Giovanni, the second from the Cathedral.

The RELIQUARY OF ST SIMEON STYLITES, in silver and gilded and embossed copper, consists of two distinct portions, made at different periods and later joined. The older portion is the base, a hexagonal urn with six square crystal windows decorated with rows of little arches; on it rests a double-stepped foot, decorated with plant motifs and piercing. The stem, embossed with nodes and cornices, supports a base for four baroque columns carrying a *cu-*

B.3

C.1

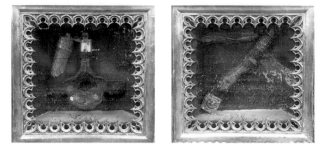

Below, the reliquary of St Simeon Stylites. The inscription engraved on the base records the donation of the relics by Charlemagne, which took place when the emperor *restituit civitatem Florentinam*. This refers to the tradition (now known to be baseless) that Charlemagne 'refounded' Florence after it had been razed to the ground by Totila (or Attila), and restored civilisation after centuries of barbarism. In reality the relics contained in the base, all of Eastern origin, came from the Grioni donation and were intended for the present base of the reliquary of St Philip the Apostle, which presumably contains the Carolingian ones. Above, details of two compartments of the base. Opposite, the reliquary of the Holy Apostles and the reliquary of a finger-bone of St John the Baptist.

pola and enclosing the crystal cylinder which contains the relics of the Saint.

The urn that forms the base, dated 1398, may be ascribed to the goldsmith Matteo di Lorenzo, who at that very time (1397-1398) was making various reliquaries to contain the relics from the Grioni donation (→ p. 139): it may be the twin of the one now used as the base for the reliquary of the arm of St Philip. The little voluted feet were probably added by Bernardo Holzman in the early 18th century. According to the Latin inscription on the base, the relics of various saints preserved in the urn were donated to the city by Charlemagne and were kept in the altar of St John, but the present contents no longer correspond to the original ones.

The upper portion (foot, stem and *cupola*) dates from the later 15th century, but the baroque voluted columns are probably another 18th-century addition by the restorer Holzman.

Next comes the RELIQUARY OF THE HOLY APOSTLES. Of gilded copper, it consists of a hexagonal *tempietto* with crystal windows and Doric columns; the *cupola* is surmounted by a voluted lantern. The stem, finely embossed and pierced, bears on the largest node the name of the donor, Niccolò Bartolini, allowing us to date the reliquary to the mid-15th century. However, the form of the *tempietto* suggests the late 16th century, so this is probably another example of those readjustments and rearrangements frequently encountered with these kinds of objects. A description of 1676 also mentions six small angels of gilded copper: they have now disappeared, and it is not at all clear where they were attached.

Some of the relics (fragments of bone from the Apostles St Andrew and St James, and from St Brice, Bishop of Tours; a splinter from the rock of Calvary) were taken from the high altar of the Baptistery after the flood of 1557, and reordered by the provost Orazio Berindelli

C.2

(1596). In the early 19th century relics of the Apostles St Peter and St Paul, and of the Blessed Ippolito Galantini, were added to them.

The third object in this case is the RELIQUARY OF A FINGER-BONE OF ST JOHN THE BAPTIST, in silver and gilded copper.   C.3

Dating from the later 15th century, it is embossed work by an unknown master; the polylobed foot and the lower portion of the splendid stem, in the form of a prism, are finely chased. The circular *tempietto* containing the relic rests on a support in the form of a vase with twisted stem, and is surmounted by a *cupola* divided into six segments, resting on three slim columns. The cast statuette of the Baptist which surmounts the lantern is somewhat similar to the one on the reliquary of the Passion, or of the 'Libretto' (→ pp. 137-138).

According to St Antoninus, Archbishop of Florence, the relic of St John the Baptist was brought in 1392 by Pepo di Arnoldo di Lapo Ruspi, who acquired it in Constantinople from a *domestikós* (palace official) of the Eastern emperor.

CASE D contains three objects. The first is a late 15th-century RELIQUARY CASKET of partially gilded silver, embossed and partly cast, covered with *pietre dure*. The work of an unknown master, it comes from the Baptistery and curiously echoes the shape of the Medici tomb carved by Andrea del Verrocchio in the Old Sacristy of the church of San Lorenzo.   D.1

Next to it is a PROCESSIONAL CROSS of gilded copper, also of the later 15th century, gothic in design but decorated with figures in the classical manner which have suggested an attribution to the circle of Luca della Robbia.   D.2

Beside the cross is an elegant RELIQUARY CASKET in enamelled and gilded silver and rock crystal. It is Venetian work, dating from the earlier 15th century.   D.3

CASE E contains three more reliquaries, the first two from the Cathedral and the third from the Baptistery.

The RELIQUARY OF ST REPARATA is of silver and gilded copper. This too is a composite work: the stem with its large central node, the foot, the lantern and the pinnacle surmounted by a lobed cross are the work of the goldsmith Francesco Vanni (last quarter of the 14th century), whereas the cylindrical crystal container with silver fastenings is an 18th-century addition. The relic came to Florence in the early 16th century from Colle Valdelsa, and was do-   E.1

In the catalogue of the Museum Brunetti ascribed the front of the processional Cross (right) to the late Luca della Robbia (who as a young man trained as a goldsmith) and the back to Antonio di Salvi Salvucci. But the debate is still open: it has been pointed out that collaborating artists do not usually divide the work so neatly and clearly. We know for certain that the Opera requested the model for a cross from Bastiano di Domenico di Bernardetto, Antonio di Salvi Salvucci and Michelangelo di Viviano. The first was paid for the model but the commission was awarded to the other two (1514). By Antonio di Salvi Salvucci, pupil of Pollaiolo and trusted goldsmith of the Opera, we have seen the reliquary of St Jerome, the *Banquet of Herod* on the Silver Altar and the reliquary of St Anthony Abbot. Michelangelo di Viviano, whose workshop "was held to be, and was, the best in Florence" (Vasari), was a pupil of Benvenuto Cellini. Since this one is the only cross to come from the Cathedral, some scholars have proposed identifying it with the cross of the competition mentioned in the documents.

The work of FRANCESCO VANNI (who was enrolled in the guild in 1366), the reliquary of St Reparata (first on the right) was made to contain long pieces of bone; the presence of the crucifix on the pinnacle suggests that it was also intended to house fragments of the True Cross. The crystal container was probably commissioned after the donation of the relic of St Reparata. This was perhaps placed together with the others as a result of the careless reading of a label describing the relics inside as coming from Santa Reparata (the church, not the saint). Beside, the reliquary of the arm of St Justus. On the opposite page, below, the two reliquary casks displayed in case D. The first (left), in enamelled and gilded silver and rock crystal, dates from the first half of the 15th century; the second (right), in parcel-gilt silver and semi-precious stone, is of the late 15th century. This latter casket was attributed to Vittore Ghiberti (son of Lorenzo) on the basis of a payment in his favour dated 1476. In fact the document probably refers to another work and so does not support this attribution; but in any case the workmanship is to be dated around that time: many details of the casket (the volutes on the top, the acanthus leaves at the corners, the lion's feet at the base) reveal the marked influence of the sarcophagus of Piero the Gouty and Giovanni de' Medici made by Andrea del Verrocchio in 1472 in the Old Sacristy of the basilica of San Lorenzo. Commissioned by Lorenzo the Magnificent (and by his younger brother Giuliano) to honour the memory of their father and uncle, Verrocchio's monument was highly admired and became a source of inspiration for an entire generation of artists. The particular polychrome effect which in the sarcophagus had been achieved by the use of different materials (porphyry, bronze, white marble, green serpentine) is here obtained by the covering in *pietre dure*.

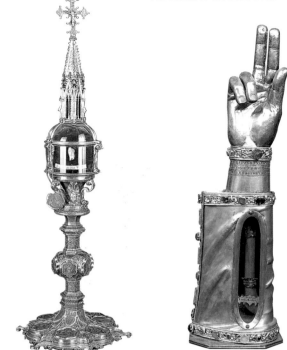

nated to the Cathedral by Cosimo della Gherardesca, a noble Florentine who had become bishop of that important border-town between Florence and Siena. Until then the only relic of St Reparata venerated in the Cathedral was an arm, donated by the Neapolitan royal family; but unfortunately when it was removed from its container, to be placed in a more precious one, it turned out to be an imitation arm made of wood and plaster.

The RELIQUARY OF THE ARM OF ST JUSTUS, in partially gilded   E.2
silver, is French work of the later 13th century, and represents the Saint's right arm with the hand raised in benediction. On the sleeve, decorated with various gems, two antique cameos are set: the upper one shows a nymph with a seated satyr playing a flute outside a temple (possibly of Isis); the lower one, attached to the base, is of chalcedony and shows a bearded man in profile.

In the 14th century this curious object, containing a relic of the sainted bishop of Lyons, was donated by the nuns of the monastery of Saint Just in Lyons to their Florentine sisters in the monastery of San Giusto alle Mura; from there it passed to the Jesuats of the convent of the Calza, until in 1680 Archbishop Nerli eventually presented it to the Cathedral.

After its great period in the 15th century, Florentine goldsmithery seems to have suffered a decline in the early 16th; this appears to have affected artistic originality, so that the more challenging or valuable pieces tended to be commissioned elsewhere, e.g. from Milan. A notable exception to the general stagnation of Florentine production is the reliquary of the 'Libretto' (opposite), which Liscia Bemporad has called "a revolutionary object". Its maker, PAOLO DI GIOVANNI SOGLIANI, is documented in the service of the Opera in the early years of the 16th century; it is possible that in 1484 he had followed his master Antonio del Pollaiolo to Rome, returning to Florence after Antonio's death in 1498. The 'Libretto', i.e. the tiny polyptych in gold decorated with enamels, rubies and pearls, had been brought to Italy by the Duke of Anjou. After many years in which all trace of it is lost, it reappears in the inventory of "jewels and other things of value" belonging to Piero the Gouty (1465), where it is described as "a tabernacle of gold with relics, ornamented with 14 rubies and pearls, i.e. with 8 pearls and 6 rubies", worth 1500 florins. Having passed into the possession of Lorenzo the Magnificent, the object is mentioned in the inventory compiled after his death (1492), but was then ceded to Francesco Piccolomini (the future Pius III) to extinguish a credit of over 9,000 florins in his favour at the Medici bank in Rome. It was from him that the Calimala repurchased the relic in 1495. Fearing that the object, which had been placed in the altar of San Giovanni, might suffer some damage, in 1499 the consuls of the Calimala decided to protect the "most beautiful and worthy relic possessed by this city of Florence", and commissioned from Sogliani this "little temple". Displayed on the Silver Altar until the mid-19th century, the reliquary was moved to the Museum in 1886, where it has been on display since 1954.

The RELIQUARY OF THE PASSION AND OF VARIOUS SAINTS, more usually known as the RELIQUARY OF THE 'LIBRETTO', is not only the most precious in the Museum but also the most curious, because the more recent container encloses an earlier one. This is a reliquary within a reliquary. E.3

We begin by examining the outer container, made by the goldsmith Paolo di Giovanni Sogliani around 1500. It is of parcel-gilt, embossed and partially cast, decorated with enamels. The quadrilobed foot – bearing on two sides the arms of the Calimala Guild, patrons of the Baptistery – ends in a square node supporting not a stem but a corbel with four volutes, bearing a rectangular aedicule of typical renaissance design. The two principal faces of this *tempietto* are flanked by pilasters, and have panels at the top containing enamel roundels of the four Evangelists: St John and St Mark on the front, St Luke and St Matthew on the back. An arched pediment rests on the entablature supported by the pilasters: the lunettes on both sides contain the same enamelled representation of the Man of Sorrows flanked by two kneeling angels. At the corners of the pediment are four small cast eagles, symbols of the Calimala; at the top, a statuette of St John the Baptist.

Inside the *tempietto* is a parcel-gilt vase from which two acanthus leaves emerge: these, together with two kneeling angels, support the 'Libretto', the earlier reliquary. French work of the later 14th century, it consists of a small foldable polyptych of gold decorated with enamels, pearls and rubies. The upper portion of the central compartment has a miniature painted on parchment, showing on the front the Crucifixion with the Virgin, St John the Evangelist and St Mary Magdalene, and on the back the Blessed Trinity with portraits of Charles V and his wife Jeanne of Bourbon. On the front are six lateral compartments – each of which is divided into four rows of three trilobed openings, containing altogether seventy-two relics of saints – and a central one containing the most important relics.

These memorials of the Passion and death of Christ were given in 1247 by the Eastern emperor Baldwin II to St Louis IX of France, who in order to house them built, near his own castle on the Ile de la Cité, Paris, the magnificent Sainte-Chapelle.

Around 1370 Charles V of Anjou had some of the fragments placed in the 'Libretto' as a gift for his brother Louis, Duc d'Anjou. Louis died at Bisceglie near Bari in

Right, the central compartment of the 'Libretto', which contains the most important relics: a fragment of the Crown of Thorns, a fragment of the Cross, and 'remains' from the Instruments of the Passion (the chains and scourge used for the Flagellation, the Lance, the purple mantle, the sponge, etc.); these latter are represented in enamel on the central panel. The history of these relics is an adventurous one.

Literally surrounded by Greeks and Bulgars and utterly penniless, the Eastern emperor Baldwin II Porphyrogenitus decided to sell the relics in his possession to the highest bidder in order to fill the state coffers (the money was not enough: in 1261 Constantinople fell into the hands of Michael VIII Palaeologus). St Louis IX of France acquired them from the Venetians (who were creditors of Baldwin and held them in a pledge) and built the Sainte-Chapelle to house it: that jewel of gothic architecture seems to have cost him rather less than the relics themselves. Over a hundred years later they were presented by King Charles V to his brother Louis, the first Duc d'Anjou, as is stated in the inscription on the back of the reliquary. In 1368 the Libretto does not appear in the inventory of jewels owned by Louis; the gift was therefore made later, possibly in 1371, when Charles presented another fragment of the True Cross, also from the Sainte-Chapelle, to another of his brothers, the Duc de Berry. The love of beautiful things was a family trait: Charles' collection of precious objects (of which the Libretto is one of the few surviving pieces) was famous, as too was the extraordinary library which he assembled in the Louvre. The Duc de Berry, best known today for the Books of Hours he commissioned – including the celebrated *Très Riches Heures* – was perhaps the greatest collector of all time: he spent fortunes on his many castles, precious stones, valuable fabrics, exotic animals and rare books.

1384, leaving the precious object in Italy. It then disappears from view until 1465, when we find it listed among the possessions of Piero the Gouty, the father of Lorenzo the Magnificent. With the expulsion of the Medici in 1494 it was confiscated by the Republic and awarded to the Calimala.

CASE F. The upper part contains a most beautiful object, unique of its kind, made in the early 14th century by extremely skilled Byzantine mosaicists.

These are two portable tablets – originally joined together to form a diptych – showing twelve scenes relating to the GREAT CHRISTIAN FEASTS. The scenes on the left represent the *Annunciation*, the *Nativity*, the *Presentation in the Temple*, the *Baptism*, the *Transfiguration* and the *Raising of Lazarus*; those on the right show the *Entry into Jerusalem*, the *Crucifixion*, the *Descent into Limbo*, the

Below, the first of the two portable Byzantine tablets showing scenes representing the *Great Christian festivals*, with its double frame: the first in embossed silver, decorated with plant motifs in enamel and gold; the second, the outer one, in carved and gilded wood, dating from the late-15th century (on the back is a painting of the Calimala eagle grasping a bale in its claws).
On the following pages, details from the tablets, with the twelve mosaic scenes. Having originally dated them to the 10th or 11th century, scholars now think – on the basis of comparison with other portable icons, mosaic cycles and miniatures – that a more likely date would be the first half (perhaps the first quarter) of the 14th century.
Del Migliore, who says that his source is St Antoninus, states that they were "taken when John Cantacuzene was driven from the empire by his son-in-law John Palaeologus and became a monk"; since Cantacuzene lost his throne in 1354, that date could well be considered the *terminus ad quem* for the making of the tablets. Of the highest artistic value – they have been called "the masterpiece of Byzantine portable mosaic" (Grabar) and "the most celebrated portable mosaics of the second golden age of Byzantine art" (Rossi) –, the mosaics are made up of minute tesserae (gold for the backgrounds, vitreous paste for the figures) set into a thin layer of wax. "The virtuosity of execution is such", writes Annamaria Giusti, "that is very difficult to understand how these subtly pictorial effects were achieved without the use of the brush". Each scene is labelled in Greek at the top. The letters bear accents and aspirates, which of course did not exist in ancient times but were introduced during the Alexandrian period to assist students in the correct pronunciation of words. Twice a year the tablets were exposed on the Silver Altar, together with the other reliquaries.

Ascension, *Pentecost* and the *Death of the Virgin*. The making of these panels was an astonishing technical feat, requiring hundreds of thousands of tesserae (gold, glass and lapis lazuli) – some no more than a few tenths of a millimetre square – fixed onto a wooden support by a layer of wax. The original frame is of embossed and partially enamelled silver.

In 1394 this magnificent object, originally from Constantinople, was presented to the Baptistery by the Venetian widow of the Florentine noble Antonio di Pietro Torrigiani, Nicoletta Grioni. Pietro Torrigiani had for some years been secretary to the Eastern emperor John Cantacuzene, and had brought the diptych back to Florence together with several precious relics which also became part of the Treasure of San Giovanni. In order to display the mosaic tablets on the silver altar-dossal on religious and civic feasts, the Calimala commissioned in the late 15th century another frame of carved and gilded wood, the back of which is painted with their symbol, the eagle and the bale of cloth: we see it in the lower part of the case.

Florence was the favourite subject of the miniaturists in the cathedral choir-book cycle. In some cases the references to contemporary reality are purely symbolic: in the page reproduced on p. 126, for example, the border displays a collection of institutional coats of arms (the traditional Florentine lily, the lion of the Republic or Marzocco, the cross of the People, the angel of the cathedral Chapter, and the lamb of the Wool Guild), and renders due homage to the Medici (the lions and bear play with their emblem's famous balls, near a laurel bush which is the device of Lorenzo the Magnificent). Elsewhere, the artists painted views of their city: having devised the intricate network of symbols just described, in the same antiphonary (Cod. C n. 11) MONTE DI GIOVANNI painted as the background to the *Marriage Feast of Cana* (right, fol. 87r) Piazza San Marco as he saw it from the window of his house, on the corner with Via Larga (now, Via Cavour). A view of the entire city is visible on the right of the mosaic showing the *Bust of St Zenobius* (opposite). Together with his brother Gherardo, who was also a famous miniaturist, Monte di Giovanni worked for many years on commissions for noble families. For the Opera he illuminated a series of choir-books and missals for the Cathedral, and he took part in the scheme to decorate the Chapel of St Zenobius with mosaic. This scheme, dear to Lorenzo the Magnificent (to one who objected that there were no longer masters of the forgotten art of mosaic, he replied: "We have so much money, we'll make some"), was suspended on his death. When it was decided to resume work (1504), Domenico Ghirlandaio and Monte's brother Gherardo were dead, and Botticelli had retired. The competition held between David and Monte was won by the latter with his *St Zenobius*. Vasari thought the mosaic to be the work of Gherardo; the correct attribution is due to Milanesi.

CASE G contains an early 16th-century glass-paste mosaic panel showing the BUST OF ST ZENOBIUS, by the miniaturist and painter Monte di Giovanni. The Saint is shown giving his blessing, dressed as bishop with mitre, crosier and cope. The latter has a figured border and is decorated with imitation gems; the large morse, consisting of a silver plate, is painted with the Florentine lily. In the background there is a rocky landscape on the left, and a view of the city on the right.

Enclosed in a contemporary frame of gilded wood, the panel dates from 1504, when the Opera commissioned from Monte and from David Ghirlandaio two alternative projects for the mosaic decoration of the Chapel of St Zenobius in the Cathedral. The model we see was preferred, and Monte received the not inconsiderable sum of one hundred gold florins. However, the mosaic decoration – which, begun in 1491 by Domenico and David Ghirlandaio, Sandro Botticelli and Gherardo di Giovanni, was also to have involved the dome (→ p. 155) – was never completed.

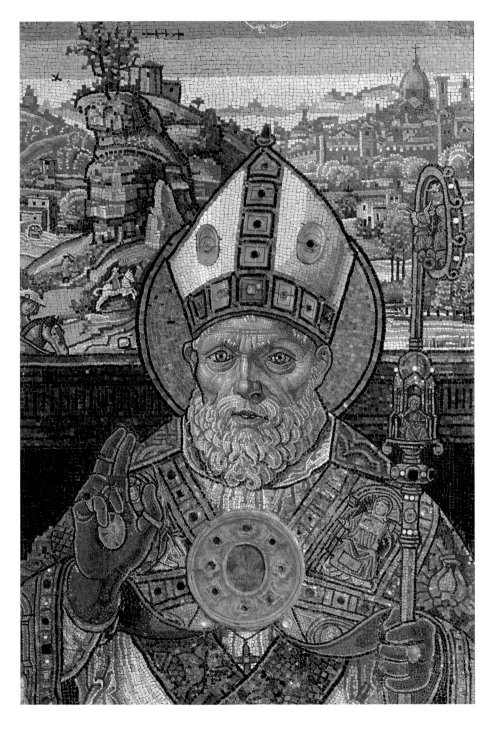

The twenty-seven 'panels' embroidered in gold and coloured silks with scenes from the life of the Baptist have the art-historical importance of a cycle of paintings, on account of their unprecedented iconographic complexity and completeness, and as a record of the artistic development of ANTONIO DEL POLLAIOLO (→ p. 124), who made the preparatory designs. The master of an entire generation, Antonio in these years devised new spatial conceptions which were to supersede the 'courtly' taste of the early Renaissance exemplified by Benozzo Gozzoli (Paolucci). His stylistic transition from chivalric elegance to an accentuated sense of drama was probably assisted by an intense meditation on the work of Donatello (especially his way of disposing figures in space and his architectural perspective), whom Antonio understood better than anyone else. The embroideries, executed by Italian, Spanish, French and Flemish workers, cost the Arte di Calimala over three thousand florins. A few years ago the Opificio delle Pietre Dure began their long and complex restoration.

The glass cases on the right wall

Crossing the room we pass on to the right wall, beginning with the glass case nearest to the silver altar and proceeding towards the exit.

The first four cases (H, I, J, K) display what is left of the magnificent EMBROIDERIES OF SAN GIOVANNI, made in the second half of the 15th century. H-K

The great religious festivals were celebrated with solemn Masses and processions and required the use of especially sumptuous vestments by the officiating priests. In 1466 the Consuls of the Calimala commissioned from Antonio del Pollaiolo designs for two dalmatics, a chasuble and a cope, showing scenes from the life of St John the Baptist. For the embroidering of Pollaiolo's designs a number of Italian and foreign (especially Flemish and French) master embroiderers were called upon, on separate occasions: Paolo di Bartolomeo from Verona, Piero di Piero from Venice, Antonio di Giovanni from Florence, Coppino di Giovanni from Malines in Brabant, Paul of Antwerp, Niccolò di Jacopo from France, Giovanni di Morale, Giovanni di Jacopo and Giovanni di Pelaio from Prignana.

This enormous labour, executed in coloured silks stitched to horizontally woven gold thread, certainly required many years: twenty-two (1466-1488), judging from the payments recorded in favour of the painter. The embroiderers succeeded remarkably well in rendering the stylis-

Opposite, the *Annunciation to Zacharias*. Above, the *Nativity* and *Circumcision* of the Baptist. Below, a detail of the *First Preaching of the Baptist*. The embroidery *a punto serrato* (as Vasari calls it) is so fine as to render the warp and weft invisible, allowing the subtle modulations characteristic of painting: an amazing technical ability which Vasari ascribes in particular to Paolo da Verona, "divine in that profession".

tic characteristics of Pollaiolo's designs, even though there are some variations in quality, inevitable in a project involving so many craftsmen.

After centuries of use, even infrequent use, the embroideries began to show signs of wear. They were then simply displayed on the silver altar, and not worn by the priests. In the 18th century the radical step was taken of dismounting the embroideries and gluing the figurative portions onto wooden panels. The cycle deals with all the episodes in the life of the Baptist, which in the four cases are presented in a hypothetical order, grouping the embroideries according to the vestments of which they once formed part. The numbers before the scenes refer to the chronological order of the episodes.

CASE H. On the left, from the top: 6. *The meeting of the Baptist with the publicans*; 18. *The arrest of the Baptist*; 19. *The Baptist is led to prison*; 20. *The Baptist is visited in prison by his disciples*.

On the right, from the top: 27. *The descent into Limbo*; 22. *The beheading of the Baptist*; 23. *The head of the Baptist is presented to Herodias*; 25. *The translation of the body of the Baptist*; 26. *The burial of the Baptist*.

Above, *the Baptist rebukes Herod.* Below, a detail of the *Meeting with the High Priest.* Opposite, the *Naming of the Baptist.* Open at the sides but equipped with sleeves, the dalmatic is worn by the bishop at high Mass and by deacons at Mass and Benediction. It takes its name from a particular type of tunic introduced to ancient Rome from Dalmatia, a region of Croatia.

CASE I. These embroideries probably come from one of the two dalmatics, where they were stitched onto the sleeves and the central panel of the front and back. On the front (left, from the top) there were: 11. *The Baptist before the priests and levites*; 10. *The Baptist before the high priest*; 14. *The Baptist points out Christ to the multitude*; 15. *The Baptist reproves Herod.* On the back (right, from the top) there were: 17. *Herodias accuses the Baptist*; 21. *The dance of Salome*; 24. *The banquet of Herod.*

CASE J. These embroideries are from the other dalmatic. On the front (left, from the top) there were: 15. *The Baptist meets Jesus*; 9. *The Baptist preaches to the multitude.* On the back (right, from the top) there were: 16. *Jesus baptises the Baptist*; 13. *The Baptist announces Christ's mission to the Pharisees*; 8. *The baptism of the neophytes.*

CASE K. These embroideries are from the chasuble, where they were arranged along the central panel. On the front (left) there were: 2. *Zacharias receives the announcement of the birth of the Baptist*; 12. *Zacharias emerges from the Temple*; 1. *The Visitation.* On the back (right) there were: 3. *The birth of the Baptist*; 4. *Zacharias writes the Baptist's name*; 5. *The circumcision of the Baptist.*

In the lower part of the case are some fragments of another set of embroidered silk vestments, attributed to Giovanni Balducci known as Cosci (late 16th century).

CASE L. In the centre, the COPE FROM THE SET OF ST REPARA- L.1
TA, Tuscan work of the 17th century. This liturgical vestment, like the others belonging to the same set (a dalmatic, two stoles, a maniple and a burse for the corporal), is of
brocade embroidered with coloured silks, gold and silver.
It was worn for the High Mass celebrated on 8 October,
the feast of St Reparata, the co-patron of the city, to whom
the old cathedral was dedicated.

On the right, the CROSIER OF BISHOP CORSINI (ca. 1425), in L.2
gilded bronze with translucent enamels from the workshop of Lorenzo Ghiberti. It belonged to the bishop A-
merigo Corsini (d. ca. 1430) and was given to the Cathedral in 1441.

CASE M. The upper part contains the CHASUBLE from the M.1
set of St Reparata (→ L). In the lower part are three liturgical objects.

The first is a BASIN of embossed, gilded copper and en- M.2
graved silver. Dateable to the first half of the 15th century,
the vessel is enriched with decorations (the three poppies,
the heraldic device of the Bartolini family) which closely
resemble those on the older portion of the reliquary of the
Holy Apostles. It is therefore probable that both objects
were made on the same occasion and for the same patrons.

Next to a German CUP in embossed and gilded copper, M.3 made in Augsburg in the early 17th century, we see a most beautiful CHALICE in gilded copper and silver (first quarter M.4 of the 16th century). The foot bears the Medici arms surmounted by a cardinal's hat: it would seem that the chalice belonged to Giulio de' Medici, Archbishop of Florence from 1513 to 1523 before ascending the papal throne as Clement VII.

CASE N contains a DALMATIC from the set of Santa Reparata ($\rightarrow$ L). N

CASE O contains the CHASUBLE OF ODOARDO FARNESE (1598- O 1600). The vestment – in satin embroidered in flat stitch and in relief, with painted silver appliqués – is decorated with volutes of acanthus supported by angels in flight. The crosses on the front and back are ornamented with medallions: those on the front show God the Father, St Paul, St Peter and, at the bottom, St Odoardus and St Hermengild; the ones on the back show the lilies and motto of Alessandro Farnese, a half-unicorn, the hyacinths and motto of Odoardo Farnese and, at the bottom, his coat of arms. The set, which is enriched by the figures painted by Annibale Carracci, also comprises an altar-frontal, of similar design; both of them were made for Cardinal Odoardo Farnese to be used in the chapel he had built at the hermitage of Camaldoli in the Casentino, chosen by the Farnese family for their private devotions. They belong to the Accademia delle Arti del Disegno, which has placed them on loan to the Opera since the opening of the Museum (1891).

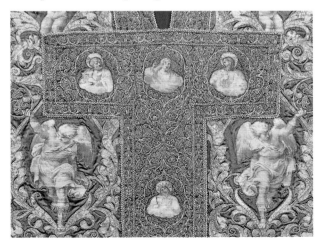

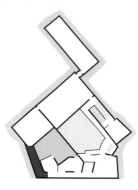

Above, BENEDETTO BUGLIONI, *St Mary of Egypt*, glazed terracotta. Below and opposite, some designs of machines devised and used by BRUNELLESCHI during the construction of the dome. "The ancients", wrote Giorgio Vasari, "never went so high with their buildings, nor did they risk challenging the sky; for it truly appears that this building challenges the heavens, rising to such a height that it seems to measure up to the hills around Florence. And it seems indeed that heaven is envious, since every day it is struck by lightning, so it appears that its fame has conquered the height of the air". The dome of the Cathedral, the largest ever built without centering, weighs 37,000 metric tons. Its construction, which required over 4,000,000 bricks, was an unprecedented feat of engineering, made possible by the futuristic machines designed by Brunelleschi on the spot. These contraptions, of which the great architect left neither drawings nor descriptions, are documented in sketches made by engineers such as FRANCESCO DI GIORGIO (right, the motor of Brunelleschi's three-speed hoist), LEONARDO DA VINCI (opposite, above, a transportable and revolving elevator from the *Codex Atlanticus*), Lorenzo Ghiberti's nephew BONACCORSO GHIBERTI (opposite, below, a revolving crane for the almost completed lantern), Mariano di Jacopo known as Taccola and Giuliano da Sangallo.

As we leave the Room of the Silver Altar, we see above the door a glazed terracotta by Benedetto Buglioni showing ST MARY OF EGYPT *(ca. 1490-1500). We cross the Room of the Cantorie and the Room of the Panels from the Campanile. At the end on the left is the entrance to the recently re-structured rooms. Our visit begins with the work-site of Filippo Brunelleschi.*

14. The work-site of Brunelleschi

In this passageway, newly arranged, we see some of the objects associated with the construction of Brunelles-

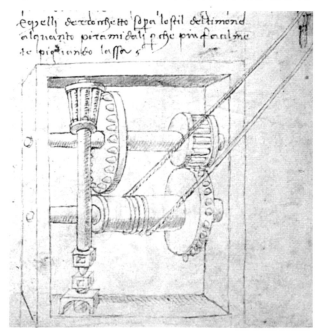

chi's dome, which the humanist architect Leon Battista Alberti described as "a structure so great, rising above the skies, big enough to cover with its shadow all the peoples of Tuscany". In this imaginary reconstruction of the work-site we see scaffolding (on the left wall) and some of the building tools used at the time (mainly displayed on the right wall): pulleys, lewises, stretchers, self-locking pincers, tackle, ropes, and moulds of various kinds for brick-making.

The fixed pulley (*taglia*) is a simple device for raising light weights; as part of a system of fixed and mobile pulleys it can be used to multiply muscle-power. The lewis is one of the earliest contrivances for raising heavy blocks of stone; the iron wedges were driven under the blocks to make traction safer. The tackle for raising weights consisted of two *bozzelli* – one fixed and one mobile – hollowed out to take the pulleys; it could be used to lift heavy weights slowly.

As early as 1357 – when the cathedral works were under the direction of Francesco Talenti and Giovanni di Lapo Ghini – it was officially decided to construct a dome, the diameter of which was to be 62 or 72 Florentine braccia (36 or 42 metres); Ghini built the drum, which was octagonal like the Baptistery. In 1367 a committee of experts, the so-called "eight masters and painters", designed an octagonal dome 144 braccia (84 metres) high and 72 (42 metres) wide: in the following year a directive obliged the members of the Opera and any future heads of the cathedral works to respect this master-plan.

From then on two separate tendencies began to emerge: the first, deriving from the gothic tradition, envisaged buttresses and pointed arches; the second, which ushered in the Renaissance, derived from classical antiquity. The discussions eventually became purely academic, however, because there remained an almost insurmountable technical problem: how to close the space?

According to the system in use in the Middle Ages, a dome under construction had to be supported by wooden centering; but given the vast size of the building, not all the forests of the Casentino would have been able supply the necessary timber.

In his *Lives of the Artists* Giorgio Vasari describes some of the proposals considered by the Opera. One ingenious person suggested hiring an army of excavators, who would fill the entire drum with earth. Then, as the dome was raised, more earth would be added, until it was all finished. The first phase would be very expensive, but the second phase – getting rid of the earth – would be simplicity itself, thanks to the city's poor. How? By mixing a certain quantity of gold florins, and silver coins, with the soil: nobody would be able to resist the temptation of bringing home a few barrow-loads of soil, in the hope of finding a little reward. True or false, this story – worthy of Baron Munchausen – effectively illustrates the passionate involvement of the citizenry in the question of the cathedral dome.

Meanwhile, between 1382 and 1421 the apsidal tribunes were com-

pleted. From 1404 the Opera several times asked Brunelleschi for advice, and in 1417 he embarked on an intensive study of statics and constructional technique, subjects on which the earlier committees of experts had been somewhat vague. In 1418 a competition was announced; both Lorenzo Ghiberti and Filippo Brunelleschi entered it, along with others. Both of them proposed the use of timber, lime and brick; Brunelleschi's bricks were to be fired and Ghiberti's unfired, that is to say simply dried in the sun. Their projects were the most convincing, and so they were jointly appointed "providers" of the dome (*provisores operis cupolae construendi*), or directors of the works.

As an indication of the continuing doubts harboured by the adjudicating commission, the competition was repeated in 1420 with the participation of other artists (Giuliano d'Arrigo known as Pesello, Donatello, Nanni di Banco), but things remained more or less as before: Brunelleschi and Ghiberti were reconfirmed in their appointments, and were joined by the master builder Battista d'Antonio as administrator (to draw up contracts with suppliers, purchase materials, etc.).

Work finally began and proceeded, for good or ill, until 1433, when there was a great change. Brunelleschi could not stomach the presence of a colleague with whom he would have to share the merit for his revolutionary technical solutions, so he sought means of getting rid of Ghiberti. According to Vasari he resorted to a pretended sickness which brought the work to a halt, revealing Ghiberti's inability to proceed on his own. And indeed the great sculptor lacked the engineering and architectural skills of Brunelleschi, who on a voyage to Rome with the young Donatello had made a lengthy study of the classical domes, especially the intact one on the Pantheon of Agrippa. Thus it was that Ser Filippo came to have sole charge of the project: from then on the dome was no longer the product of shared labours, as in the medieval workshops, but became a 'work of art' in the modern sense of the term.

Building techniques and tools

The construction of the dome presented difficulties of a kind hitherto unthinkable, both technical and organisational. The most serious, that of the wooden centering, was avoided by introducing – for the first time in the modern age – the concept of a self-supporting structure: the dome bore its own weight while it was being built. The loss of almost all the original documents prevents us from understanding in detail the technical features of Brunelleschi's plan: we know however that the secret lay in the arrangement of the bricks. Instead of being laid in parallel rows they were arranged in a fish-bone pattern, providing resistance to the force of gravity essential in a curved structure.

To ensure stability it was further necessary to lighten the dome as much as possible, since if it were too heavy it would weigh dangerously on the drum. This was achieved by having an empty space between an outer and an inner dome, within which stone steps were made, leading up to the lantern.

In the course of the work it was necessary continually to check that the curvature was proceeding correctly. Very firm scaffolding was needed for safe work at such a great height. In the beginning, when the walls of the dome were still almost vertical, the scaffolding was supported by beams inserted in the special holes still visible on the exterior, but as work proceeded the increasing inclination required a different system: Brunelleschi devised a kind of scaffolding suspended in the void, placed in the centre of the dome and joined by beams to platforms fixed lower down, which were used to store materials and equipment.

The traditional medieval implements were not sufficient for raising great quantities of bricks to such an enormous height, and new devices had to be applied to the capstans and pulleys in order to multiply their lifting power. The motive force for these machines was supplied by a pair of horses or oxen turning a central vertical shaft; the torsion was transmitted to a horizontal shaft which turned the pulleys of the lifting gear.

Furthermore, Ser Filippo arranged the lighting on the stairs built between the outer and the inner dome, organised a complex system for collecting the rain-water, and even set up small kitchens so that the workmen would not have to waste time climbing up and down for meals.

The structure and the space

The dome is a fantastical architectural machine but it is also a 'spatial structure', a form representing universal space.

With his famous phrase ("a structure so great, rising above the skies, big enough to cover with its shadow all the peoples of Tuscany"), Leon Battista Alberti characterised an element that is structural in itself, and self-supporting.

The buttresses, which in gothic architecture were partially supporting elements, are here rendered homogeneous with the whole. Perspectives converge onto a point representing the infinite, so that the dome comes to represent the universe itself. This sense of space above the skies is emphasised by the drum, which allows the dome to detach itself from the rest of the building and thus to achieve an almost complete formal autonomy.

The lantern

On the summit of the dome stands the lantern. Twenty metres high, it has a conical roof and is supported by an octagonal base with eight radiating buttresses; in each of the eight faces is a tall arched window, flanked by semi-columns with acanthus-leaf capitals.

A masterpiece of stonecutting on a giant scale, the lantern reveals the close connection between the work of the architect and that of the goldsmith, whose technique was a part of every artist's apprenticeship until the early Renaissance. Like the lantern on the Tribune of the Uffizi, this 'architecture within architecture' is inspired by classical models, and especially by the Tower of the Winds in Athens, a small octagonal marble building of the 1st century BC.

Brunelleschi had envisaged a lantern in his plan submitted for the competition of 1418. Sixteen years later, when the *serraglia* or key-stone was finally set into position, a new competition was announced for the lantern. In 1436 the participants – who included Brunelleschi, Ghiberti and Antonio Manetti Ciaccheri – submitted their designs; Brunelleschi was declared the winner, but died in 1446, shortly after work begun. It dragged on for a quarter of a century, under several different architects who made alterations to the original plan. The bronze sphere for the top, commissioned from Verrocchio, was installed in 1471, though it had to be replaced when it was knocked down by a thunderbolt in 1601.

The balcony

Between 1460 and 1506 the lower part of the drum – the portion pierced by large circular windows (oculi) – was sheathed in white and green marble, like the rest of the cathedral exterior. The upper part of the drum remained bare stone, and the intention was to devise some sort of architectural element joining the drum to the base of the dome. As early as 1418 Filippo Brunelleschi had designed a balcony supported by beccatelli (small projecting arches typical of medieval fortifications) and with open-work parapets; he had even had a wooden model made of it, now lost; but so great were the technical problems that the scheme was never carried out.

After the death of Brunelleschi the idea was taken up again by Antonio Manetti Ciaccheri, in charge of the cathedral works from 1452 to 1460, who considerably modified the original scheme, as too did his successors: Giuliano da Maiano (1477-1490), Simone del Pollaiolo known as Cronaca (from 1495), and lastly Baccio d'Agnolo, Antonio and Giuliano da Sangallo. In 1507 a competition was announced; Michelangelo took part in it, but the winning model (below) was the joint submission of Cronaca, Giuliano da Sangallo and Baccio d'Agnolo, who were later joined by Antonio da Sangallo. After the death of Cronaca the designers fell out, and the Sangallos resigned, leaving Baccio d'Agnolo with the entire burden of the enterprise. And a burden it was, because the south-east section of the balcony, inaugurated in 1515, attracted far from favourable criticism. Michelangelo, famously, called it a "cage for crickets"; the scheme was abandoned, and no more of it was ever built.

The internal decoration

We know that the problem of the internal decoration of the dome was of the greatest importance to Brunelleschi. It would be necessary to make the most of the fairly meagre light entering from the windows in the drum and from the lantern would have to be, and the best way of doing so would undoubtedly be to use mosaic, the technique employed by Donatello in order to minimise the effect of poor lighting on his Cantoria (→ pp. 108-109 and 114). Furthermore, mosaic decoration would be in harmony not only with the original façade but also with the interior of the Baptistery, creating an ideal correspondence between the two great symbols of

the religious spirit of Florence. It was to assist the work of the mosaicists that Brunelleschi had left the scaffolding-holes in the segments of the vault; unfortunately his death in 1446 put an end to the project, and the inside of the dome was simply whitewashed. More than a century later Duke Cosimo I decided to have the vault painted. The work was begun in 1568 by Giorgio Vasari and his assistants, and completed in 1579 by Federico Zuccari and a number of collaborators, including Domenico Cresti known as Passignano. The quality of this enormous fresco, which represents the *Last Judgement*, is very uneven, both because of the variety of artists who took part, and because of the different techniques used (true fresco for Vasari's part, and painting *a secco* for Zuccari's); but above all the style looks incongruous in that vast dome, where Brunelleschi had wanted the shadowy vaults to glimmer with refulgent gold.

Right, the wooden model for the lantern of the dome. Badly damaged during the 1966 flood, it has now been fully restored. But is it really the model presented by Filippo Brunelleschi for the competition of 1436? The model, which bears the date 1673, differs in several minor respects from the finished lantern. Then there is the question of the staircase: according to Vasari, the architect had provided his model with an internal staircase for climbing up to the ball, concealing it with "a little inlaid wood"; the judges declared that, had it not been for the lack of the staircase, they would undoubtedly have chosen Brunelleschi; whereupon he removed the cover, revealed his staircase and was proclaimed the winner. Sanpaolesi, who attributed the model to Filippo and considered it more perfect than the finished lantern, had to explain why there was no staircase in it: at first he regarded Vasari's story as fictional; later he proposed that the construction of the staircase was one of the modifications requested by the judges. Luisa Becherucci has developed a different hypothesis. Over the centuries the lantern has been struck at least eighteen times by lightning; the particularly severe instance of 27 January 1601 is documented in Alessandro Allori's drawing on the opposite page. The Grand Duke Ferdinando I entrusted the reconstruction to Allori, Buontalenti and Gherardo Mechini, specifying that the lantern was to be rebuilt exactly as before; his inspectors were to search the city for drawings or plans. And why should they need to do that – asks Becherucci – if the model already existed? According to her, our model is a reproduction not intended for construction (which explains the absence of the staircase) and was made in the later 17th century (which explains the date) by the architects and engineers charged with "supervising the constantly threatened lantern".

15. The corridor

After the reconstruction of the work-site the passage of Brunelleschi turns left.

Just at the corner we see the MODEL OF THE LANTERN OF THE DOME, made of wood to Brunelleschi's design. It probably dates from 1436, when the dome had been completed with an octagonal platform on top, and a competition was held for the design of the lantern (→ pp. 155-156).

To us it seems extraordinary that an architectural and engineering genius like Brunelleschi should be compelled to enter a competition in order to be awarded the commission for what was after all a purely ornamental addition to his dome.

The fact is that the regulations of the corporations insisted on formal public competitions. We are at the transitional point between two eras and two different ways of regarding the artist's activity: on the one hand, the medieval period with its anonymous artisans; on the other, the dawning Renaissance with its creative genius, who alone signs the work.

The octagonal lantern is joined to the marble ribbing of the dome by the ring at its summit. Instead of the dichromatic alternation he used on other occasions (marble and brick, grey stone and white plaster), Brunelleschi here preferred the "absolute white" of marble, which confers on the structure "a sense of immaterial lightness" (Fanelli). The great architect thus achieved a perfect synthesis between the static function of the lantern (to press down on the dome, squashing it) and its figurative function ("it intensifies to the maximum, at the vanishing-point of all the lines of thrust, the exchange between full and void"). Below right, the death-mask of Filippo Brunelleschi. The bust by Buggiano, who used this mask as a model, stands in the first bay of the Cathedral's right aisle, above the tomb of Brunelleschi which was discovered in the crypt of Santa Reparata; it bears a Latin inscription by Carlo Marsuppini.

Examining the model, we notice some differences from the lantern as built; for example, the model lacks the internal stairs, which were probably requested by the commission that judged the competition.

On the left, in a glass case in an alcove, is the DEATH MASK OF FILIPPO BRUNELLESCHI (1446). His adoptive son, the sculptor and architect Andrea Cavalcanti known as Buggiano, used it as a model when in the same year he carved the marble roundel on the architect's tomb in the right nave of the Cathedral.

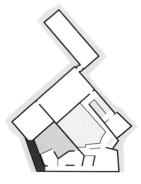

Above, the left wall of the balcony room with the models by ANDREA SANSOVINO; ANTONIO DA SANGALLO; SIMONE DEL POLLAIOLO, BACCIO D'AGNOLO, GIULIANO AND ANTONIO DA SANGALLO; GIULIANO DA MAIANO; ANTONIO MANETTI. Opposite, below, the right wall with the two models by MICHELANGELO, the anonymous 15th-century model and the great model of the dome and of the apsidal portions of the Cathedral.

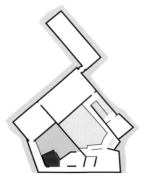

The balcony

On the same side of the corridor is a series of small rooms. In the first are a number of models for the balcony which was to have run around the drum at the base of the dome (→ p. 156).

On the left wall and on the wall opposite the entrance we see: three WOODEN MODELS for the competition of 1507, illustrating the designs by Andrea Sansovino, by Antonio da Sangallo and by Simone del Pollaiolo, Baccio d'Agnolo and Giuliano and Antonio da Sangallo; the MODEL OF GIULIANO DA MAIANO (ca. 1479); the MODEL OF ANTONIO MANETTI CIACCHERI (ca. 1460), which, as we have seen, takes up and adapts Brunelleschi's original design. 1-3 4 5

In the glass case to the right of the entrance, beginning on the left, we see: MICHELANGELO'S MODEL for the competition of 1507; a DESIGN BY MICHELANGELO produced in 1516, after the artist had already sneered at Baccio d'Agnolo's "cage for crickets"; an ANONYMOUS 15TH-CENTURY MODEL, perhaps made from a design by Brunelleschi. Between the two models by Michelangelo is a large MODEL OF THE DOME AND THE APSIDAL PORTIONS OF THE CATHEDRAL, possibly made for Brunelleschi himself. 6 8 9 7

Previously thought to have been an assemblage of different elements, the model of the dome and apsidal portions (right) seems in fact to have been conceived as a unity. Certain clues (the uniform width of the corner piers, which in fact are narrower at the level of the first cornice, and the diameter of the *oculi* which is smaller than the actual one) suggest a date earlier than 1465, that is to say before the drum was sheathed in marble; some have associated it with Brunelleschi himself (1429?), and others even with the project of the *magistri* of 1367 (⟶ p. 152).

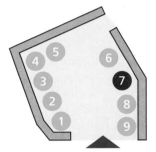

A common feature of the wooden models of the façade – apart from the difficulty of identifying their makers (they have been called "seven models in search of an author") – is their contemporary inspiration. It has been observed (e.g. by Cresti) that none of the projects had the courage to deal with what already existed (Arnolfo's gothic cathedral, Brunelleschi's dome, the Campanile): this would have meant facing problems of structural consistency (conceiving the façade in relation to the rest of the church) and spatial consistency (conceiving the façade in relation to the surrounding buildings), also in order to prevent "an excessive assemblage of elements" on the façade from creating "a clogging effect" in a piazza already crowded with the Baptistery, the Loggia del Bigallo and the Archbishop's Palace. Instead, the façade was treated as an independent entity, and the various proposals – which make use of the elements of the architectural orders by combining them in different ways – are distinguished from each other only by solutions of a purely stylistic nature: the use of two or of three orders, the adoption of single or paired columns or pilasters, and so on. Why did they ever decide to dismantle the old façade? To attribute the decision solely to the religious zeal of Francesco seems unwarranted. Some of the sources ascribe it to the Grand Duke's policy of public works set in motion to counter the abject poverty that followed the famine of 1586. Others attribute it to Bernardo Buontalenti's insistent attempts to convince Francesco of the need to equip the Cathedral with a 'modern' façade: a commission which the ambitious architect would himself have accepted with alacrity. On this occasion he did not succeed, though in 1594 he managed to have the old Romanesque façade of the church of Santa Trinita replaced by one of his own design.

The 16th- and 17th-century models for the façade

In the next room there are some models for the façade of the Cathedral.

As we have seen (→ pp. 24-25), the original unfinished façade was demolished on the orders of the Grand Duke Francesco de' Medici in the short time between 21 January and 9 July 1587. In the same year a competition was announced for the new façade, attracting all the major Tuscan artists of the time, but nobody won it, because on 19 October Francesco died of an illness so rapid as to arouse suspicions of poisoning.

After almost half a century Ferdinando II decided to press on with the project, but instead of announcing a new competition he settled on the design submitted in 1587 by Antonio Dosio. The Grand Duke's decision, taken without consulting the experts or the citizenry, provoked such ill feeling that he was constrained to turn to the Accademia delle Arti del Disegno. In 1635 the Academy's collective project, duly approved, was entrusted to Gherardo Silvani, the architect to the Opera del Duomo, who began work at once. Soon however Silvani found that he was restricted to a merely executive role, because his work was closely supervised by the President of the Academy, the sculptor Giovanni Battista Pieratti. After some sharp conflicts and tedious polemics the work ground to a halt in 1639.

Beginning on the left we see the four older MODELS 1-4 (1587), those of Giovanni Antonio Dosio, of Don Giovanni de' Medici, of Bernardo Buontalenti and of Giambologna (on its own in the case in the centre).

All influenced by Michelangelo, they are of two orders (Corinthian and Composite), except for the design by

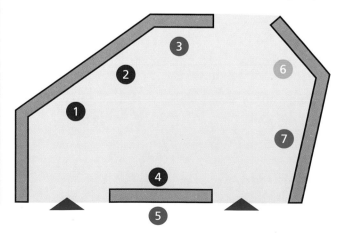

Above, BERNARDO BUONTALENTI, wooden model for the façade of Santa Maria del Fiore, 234×202 cm (inv. n. 132; the inventory numbers are those of Poggi's catalogue, 1904). This is the only 16th-century model with three orders and – unusually – critics are unanimous in attributing it to Buontalenti.

An artist more interested in decorative detail than in structure, Francesco's favourite architect excelled in designing ornamental details and objects such as vases, and in devising theatrical spectacles with much use of fireworks, stage machinery and automata. In this case too he went for effect, producing "a crowded pattern-book of ornamentation". The ensemble suffers as a result: the insistent horizontal divisions create a series of superimposed registers, unrelated to each other.

Below, GIOVANNI ANTONIO DOSIO, wooden model for the façade of Santa Maria del Fiore, 256×218 cm (inv. n. 128). Attributed in 1887 to Dosio by Luigi Del Moro, the designer of the Opera del Duomo Museum, it was ascribed by Poggi to Giovanni de' Medici on the basis of an inventory of 1697 (and of the presence of the Medici arms). Later, for stylistic reasons, and because of the description of the model found in the documents of the 1635 competition, it was re-attributed to Giovanni Dosio.

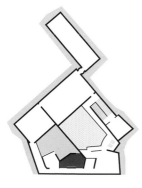

Right, GIAMBOLOGNA, wooden model for the façade of Santa Maria del Fiore, 143x120 cm (inv. n. 133). Made in the reign of the Grand Duke Ferdinando I (whose name is visible on the cornice of the first order), it was already assigned to Giambologna in the catalogue of 1891. Poggi (1904) records it as "author unknown". In the early 20th century there was a proposal to attribute it to Ludovico Cigoli: this hypothesis was revived by Matteoli, who actually sought to exclude Giambologna from the list of the authors of the models. But he was certainly responsible for the drawing used for the gold and amethyst relief above, now in the Museo degli Argenti in the Pitti Palace. The plaque shows Bernardo Buontalenti presenting Francesco with his model for the façade (possibly the very one displayed in this room, before some changes were made). From a document of 1589 it would appear that Ferdinando I, Francesco's brother and successor, preferred Dosio's model. Below, DON GIOVANNI DE' MEDICI, wooden model for the façade of Santa Maria del Fiore, 233x218 cm (inv. n. 135). Poggi thought that this model was by Giambologna, but later scholars seem to be agreed in attributing it to Don Giovanni de' Medici, the bastard son of Grand Duke Cosimo I by Leonora degli Albizzi. He was an architect, scientist, man of letters and artillery engineer. Together with Buontalenti and Matteo Nigetti he was responsible for the celebrated Chapel of the Princes, the family mausoleum attached to the church of San Lorenzo. Giovanni died in Venice in 1621.

Below, the project by the ACCADEMIA DEL DISEGNO, 250×240 cm (inv. n. 134). After Ferdinando's proposal to use Dosio's design had been set aside, the Accademia del Disegno determined that the new projects should have three orders, and after a heated debate presented its own model, which critics have at various times attributed to Baccio del Bianco, Giovan Battista Pieratti and Sigismondo Coccapani. The date of the competition, 1635, appears on the frieze of the attic entablature. Work began in October 1636, was interrupted in 1638 and suspended indefinitely the following year. In 1645 a new design was requested from the painter Pietro da Cortona.

Buontalenti (Corinthian on the lower order and Composite on the two upper ones); but in an unfinished earlier MODEL – displayed in the case facing onto the corridor – the Grand Duke's architect had adopted the same scheme as the other three.

In the glass case at the end, the TRIPLE-ORDERED PROJECT OF THE ACCADEMIA DEL DISEGNO, which we have already mentioned, is preceded by a MODEL ON PAPER by Ludovico Cigoli, produced in the same period.

Needless to say, none of these designs takes the architecture of the Cathedral into account. Despite their considerable differences, the 16th- and 17th-century projects seem inspired by a theatrical monumentality, absent from the present façade by Emilio De Fabris, which – whatever else one might say about it – is at least inspired by the Cathedral's gothic style.

The 19th-century façade of the Cathedral

The question of the façade, left unresolved after the last unfortunate attempt in 1636, was taken up again by Giovanni degli Alessandri – President of the Accademia delle Arti del Disegno, and of the Opera del Duomo – in 1822. In that year a project was presented by Giovanni Battista Silvestri; it was followed in 1831 by another by Gaetano Baccani, who had been responsible for the purist intervention on the cathedral interior. The problem was not only aesthetic, but financial. In 1842 a body was set up ('The Association for the Façade of the Cathedral') to collect the necessary funds, and a design was commissioned from Niccolò Matas, who had put the new façade on Santa Croce. His neo-gothic solution, which aroused widespread interest, emerged from a cultural climate at European level. In philosophy French spiritualism and, in some respects, German idealism were causing a general revaluation of medieval religiosity: this phenomenon affected not only historiography but also art, literature and architecture. In France, Eugène Viollet-le-Duc (1814-1879) set about restoring some of the great medieval churches (including the abbey church of Vézelay, and Notre-Dame and the Sainte-Chapelle in Paris), and wrote his great *Dictionnaire raisonné de l'architecture française du XIe au XVIe siècle*. In the same spirit the young Swiss architect Johann Georg Müller (1822-1849), who visited Florence during his protracted tour of Italy, gathered ideas from Matas and between 1843 and 1844 produced no fewer than six designs for the cathedral façade.

The three competitions
The exciting events of the Risorgimento – the first, short-lived expulsion from Tuscany of the Habsburg-Lorraine dynasty (1848), and more especially the revolution of 1859, which put an end to the Grand Dukedom and saw the birth of the Republic – naturally interrupted the plans for putting a new façade on the Cathedral.

The plebiscite of 12 March 1860 resulted in the annexation of Tuscany by the kingdom of Italy; a little over a month later, on 18 April, the Association for the Façade of the Cathedral was relaunched under a new name, the 'Promoting Deputation'. On 22 April the king of Italy, Vittorio Emanuele II, laid the first stone of the façade; it was a purely symbolic gesture, because no design had been chosen; and in fact the previously announced competition, for which entries were supposed to be in by 30 May, was annulled. On 2 May the Deputation announced another competition, with the same rules as before, fixing the expiry date for 31 December 1862. The adjudicating commission – this time, in deference to the new national unity, composed of academicians from the whole of Italy – failed to agree on a winner. A second competition was announced, to expire in April 1864, and was won by Emilio De Fabris. His design provoked violent criticism, however, not only in Italy but also abroad: the third and final competition was then announced, but its closing date (July 1866) had to be put off for two more years.

In the thirty years between the founding of the Association and this third competition, the cultural climate had undergone a profound change. With the decline of Romanticism, so strong an influence on the first part of the 19th century, increasing gains were made

by positivism, which was by definition a scientific and a lay (indeed anti-clerical) creed; moreover, the process of political unification, although supported by Catholics such as Vincenzo Gioberti, had led to increasing bitterness between the 'patriots' and the Church. This bitterness reached its acme on 20 September 1870, when the walls of Rome, last bastion of the Papal States, were breached by nationalist troops.

It is no wonder that the design of the façade – which became of national interest while Florence was temporarily capital of Italy (1865-1870) – came to assume symbolic importance far beyond aesthetic considerations: while lay opinion favoured the 'basilical' type, traditionalist Catholics clamoured for the three-pointed 'gothic' model (left, the two schemes illustrated by Niccolò Barducci).

The third competition, held against the background of these incessant polemics, was again won by Emilio De Fabris, who in January 1869 was appointed architect to the Opera, with the task of building the new façade to his own design.

Despite financial problems, which required the periodic launching of appeals to the public for more money, the new façade was presented to the world on 5 December 1883 (it would be officially inaugurated

on 12 May 1887); over the next twenty years the sculptural programme would be completed, and the bronze doors installed.

The sculptural decoration

The richness, or if you prefer the superabundance, of architectural ornament which characterises De Fabris' façade is augmented and emphasised by the sculptural decoration. In drawing up the programme of sculpture the ecclesiastical authorities sought the advice of a prominent Catholic intellectual, the historian Augusto Conti, who taught philosophy at the University. In 1878 Conti agreed with the architect a detailed iconographic plan, taking up and developing the principal theme of Arnolfo's original façade – the role of the Virgin in the economy of salvation – and linking it to the theme of the Campanile – Christianity as the driving force in human history – so as to present, in addition to subjects drawn from Sacred Scripture, a gallery of great artists, writers, scientists and politicians who distinguished themselves in the name of faith.

The work of several artists, the sculptures on the façade exemplify the evolution of Florentine figurative culture in the later 19th century, and illustrate its various tendencies, from purism to realism and the beginnings of symbolism.

After the demolition, the cathedral façade was several times painted with temporary architecture: for the marriage of Ferdinando I and Christine of Lorraine (1589) it was covered with canvases, stuccoes, paintings and statues; on the occasion of the arrival in Florence of Marguerite Louise d'Orléans (who had married Cosimo III by proxy in the Louvre), it was once again covered with canvas and adorned with medallions and bas-reliefs; in 1688, for the marriage of Cosimo's son, the Grand Prince Ferdinando, to Violante of Bavaria, the front was plastered and then painted to a design by Ercole Graziani. This decoration – right, in a 1733 engraving by Bernardo Sansone Sgrilli – would survive into the 19th century. Just for interest, we give the list of objects used for the ceremony of the laying of the first stone (22 April 1860): two vases, two cups with lids, two goblets, two jars with spouts and saucers, six saucers of French crystal; three glass cylinders; a carved and gilded wooden hand-barrow to carry the stone; a walnut mortar-board with a carved and gilded foot; a gilded iron mallet with a wooden handle; a gilded steel trowel with a wooden handle; a knife with a gilded handle; two gilded spoons; ropes to raise the stone; a galloon with the arms of Florence; gilded iron hooks for moving the stone; a plaster model of the stone; four sponges, to be used for moistening the stone with holy-water.

Fig. XIII 4

Facciata del Duomo di Firenze, come si trova presentemente dipinta

Studies for the 19th-century façade

In the next room we find some documentation on the genesis of the 19th-century façade (→ pp. 166-169). The panel on the right – presented to the Opera in 1900 by the architect Luca Beltrami – contains three AUTOGRAPH DRAWINGS by the Swiss architect Johan Georg Müller, accompanied by an ENGRAVING with a portrait of the artist, and by another in which his sixth project is compared with that of Niccolò Matas. On the left, copies of two more PENCIL DRAWINGS by Müller.

In the case opposite, there is a PHOTOGRAPH OF THE LAYING OF THE FIRST STONE (22 April 1860), and on the end wall, a series of objects used for that ceremony.

At the end of the corridor is the Room of the 19th-century Façade, which on the left faces onto the new balcony and the covered courtyard.

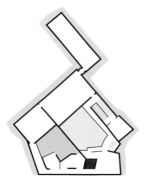

Below, a photograph taken in the 1870s, before work began on the new cathedral façade; in the background, the basilica of Santa Croce. Along the ridges of the Baptistery's pyramidal roof (lower right) run the projecting ribs which were removed in 1896 by Luigi Del Moro during work carried out to eliminate the seepage of rainwater which was ruining the ancient mosaics of the dome.

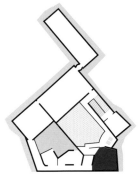

16. The Room of the 19th-century Façade

The wall to the left of the entrance has a few exhibits associated with Emilio De Fabris: at the top, in the centre, his PORTRAIT (1899), an oil on canvas by the Florentine painter and illustrator Egisto Sarri; on the left an ink and water-colour DRAWING OF THE FAÇADE, dating from 1876, when work had been proceeding for some years; to the right is another elevation of 1866-1867, prepared for the third and final competition. Below are some COMMEMORATIVE BRONZE MEDALS of the new façade and its architect, struck in the 1880s.

Opposite the corridor and at the far right of the wall devoted to De Fabris are two 19th-century sculptures by Giovanni Battista Tassara: they represent SAMUEL and AARON, and stood above the right doorway. The statues of ADAM and EVE by Lot Torelli, which stood above the left doorway, are now displayed in the balcony (see below). These statues, copies of which are now being prepared in the Opera's workshop, are presumably only the first of many which will gradually have to be removed from the façade for reasons of conservation.

Above, *portrait of Emilio De Fabris* by the Florentine EGISTO SARRI. Right, EMILIO DE FABRIS' plan for the façade of Santa Maria del Fiore which won the competition announced in 1866. During the course of work it was decided not to complete the cusps shown in this plan, and to adopt instead a basilical-type crowning proposed by De Fabris himself in another plan. Below, the triple-cusped version presented by the English architect WILLIAM BURGESS, one of the principal exponents of the Gothic Revival in the later 19th century. In the course of a long series of travels in France, Germany and Italy, Burgess visited the monuments of gothic architecture, from which he drew inspiration for his own designs (including Cork Cathedral, the *aula magna* at Harrow School and his own house in Kensington).

On the high wall opposite the corridor, interrupted half-way up by a balcony with balustrade, are displayed the designs (some of them anonymous or pseudonymous) submitted for the final competitions, and here listed in our usual order, i.e. beginning at upper left: 1. Camillo Boito, THREE-POINTED ELEVATION (1867); 2. Buscone di Milano, PINNACLED ELEVATION (1862); 3. Mariano Falcini, SINGLE-POINTED ELEVATION (1864-1866); 4. Antonio Cipolla, BASILICAL ELEVATION (1866); 5. Anonymous, using the motto 'Un nobile desìo mi spinge all'opra', SINGLE-POINTED ELEVATION (1864); 6.-7. Gaetano Baccani, SIDE VIEW OF THE FAÇADE (1860-1861); 8. Oscar Sommer, ELEVATION (1864); 9. Mariano Falcini, ELEVATION (1864); 10. Giuseppe Martelli, BASILICAL ELEVATION (1866); 11. Ferdinando Lasinio, BASILICAL ELEVATION (1868-1870); 12. Anonymous, using the motto 'Desio d'onor esser mi fece audace', BASILICAL ELEVATION (1862); 13. Anonymous, using the motto 'Santa Maria', ELEVATION (1866-1867); 14. Wilhelm Petersen,

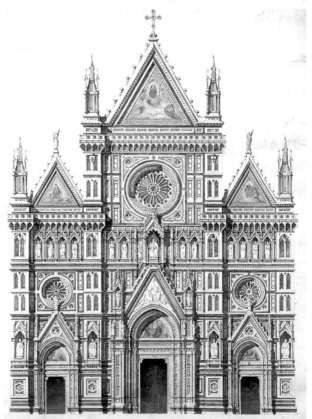

BASILICAL ELEVATION (1864); 15. Francesco Del Ry, BASILICAL ELEVATION (1875); Andrea Scala, ELEVATION WITH HORIZONTAL CROWNING (1864); 17. Alessandro Antonelli, ELEVATION WITH HORIZONTAL CROWNING (1864).

On the left wall, reduced copies of twenty-four more ELEVATIONS in pen and ink. Some of them are very far from the dominant neo-gothic academicism: notice in particular the drawing in the style of the Secession, in the third frame from the bottom, full of eclectic borrowings from exotic archaeological sources ranging from Mesopotamia to India.

In order to see the upper rows properly, you should leave the room and take the stairs overlooking the courtyard, up to the balcony.

This small room, frequently used for lectures and conferences, houses the Museum's educational section and offers a small exhibition specially designed for non-sighted visitors, consisting of reproductions, casts and models (including one of the Cathedral). In this room there are (or soon will be) – next to the statues of ADAM and EVE by Lot Torelli – a BUST OF THE REDEEMER of the Pisan school (15th century) and a polychrome terracotta by Giovanni Bandini known as Giovanni dell'Opera representing the MAGDALENE (ca. 1565). By this artist, who on the death of his master Baccio Bandinelli completed the choir of the Cathedral (→ pp. 56-57), we have already seen the bust of Cosimo I on the façade (→ p. 13), and the bust of Filippo Brunelleschi, in the Room of the Porta della Mandorla (→ p. 69).

At the time of writing two fragments of fresco from the Cathedral are not yet on display. Until 1999 they were on either side of the door leading into the Room of the Cantorie. Both fragments were detached from the wall of the Cathedral in the late 1830s, during the alterations carried out by the architect Gaetano Baccani (→ p. 44). On that occasion some frescoes were partially uncovered which had been painted between 1436 and 1440, and whitewashed by Vasari in 1569; the 'restoration', conducted with the typical criteria of the time by the painter Antonio Marini, unfortunately involved a good deal of arbitrary repainting. The first fragment is a HEAD OF ST ANDREW (1436) by Lippo d'Andrea and comes from the first chapel in the left tribune. The second one, a head of ST JUDE THADDEUS (1440), comes from the nave and is by Bicci di Lorenzo, who with the help of assistants produced a complete cycle of Apostles.

The Door of Paradise (opposite page, before restoration) was the last of the Baptistery's three doors to be made: it was preceded by Andrea Pisano's door showing *Scenes from the life of St John the Baptist*, originally installed on the east side in 1336, and by the door showing the *Life of Christ* (below), made by Ghiberti after he won the competition of 1401. In 1424 Ghiberti's first door replaced the 14th-century one at the main entrance to the Baptistery, and the Consuls of the Calimala – the guild which as we have seen held the patronage of San Giovanni – were fully conscious of its merit. They therefore decided to assign the third door to the same "excellent master", taking the highly unusual step of doing so without holding a competition.

The only restriction placed upon the artist was that he was to be held to the subject – scenes from the Old Testament – chosen by Leonardo Bruni, the Chancellor of the Republic and a learned humanist, who on the analogy of the two earlier doors had devised a sequence of twenty-eight compartments, comprising twenty Old Testament scenes and eight figures of prophets. Ghiberti must have begun work on this scheme, because the back of the door is divided into twenty-eight squares, each with a boss in the centre; but very soon the scheme was changed, probably at the instigation of the artist himself, so as to reduce as far as possible the number of the divisions and thereby obtain much larger panels. Assistance in adapting the Old Testament scenes to the new arrangement was provided by Ambrogio Traversari, general of the Camaldolese Order, who for this purpose made use of the doctrines of St Antoninus, the Archbishop of Florence (1389-1459). But Lorenzo was left free to express himself according to his taste and abilities, with an almost unlimited budget, as he says in his *Commentaries*: "I was allowed to proceed in the way that I thought would make it most perfect and most splendid and most rich".

Even the time allowed to him was generous, and indeed the completion of the doors – with the assistance of Luca della Robbia, Donatello, Michelozzo (from 1436 to 1442), Benozzo Gozzoli (from 1442), Ghiberti's own sons Vittore and Tommaso, and Bernardo Cennini – required no less than twenty-seven years of painstaking labour. In the 1429 the bronze frames were cast, which were to receive the ten reliefs; ten years later only five of the panels were ready; by 1443 there were still four panels missing, which were only completed in 1447. But the result justified every expectation: the finished door was so splendid that in 1452 the authorities decided to substitute it

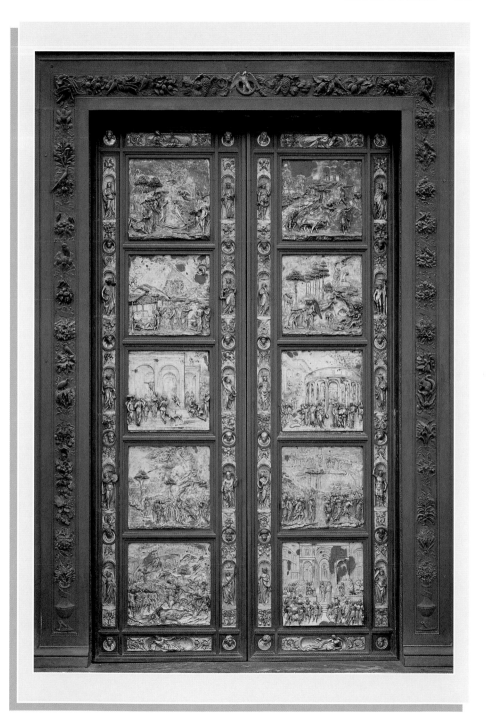

for Ghiberti's earlier door on the side facing the Cathedral, the place of honour called Paradisium. This is probably the origin of the name 'Door of Paradise', by which Ghiberti's second door is generally known; though according to another tradition, recorded by Vasari, the phrase was coined by Michelangelo.

Ghiberti's innovations

The episodes from Scripture narrated on the Door of Paradise are not broken up into a multitude of small scenes, nor are they enclosed within the traditional gothic quatrefoils; instead, they are distributed in ten large panels. This arrangement allowed Ghiberti to confer on the scenes a hitherto unknown breadth and compositional harmony, but it also presented him with a serious difficulty: how to distinguish one scene from another within the same panel? It was confusing to show simultaneously two or more events which took place at different times. Ghiberti's brilliant solution was to vary the height of the relief, so as to lend variety to the composition and also clearly to distinguish the individual episodes. This was a technical and formal solution of great originality; the creative autonomy allowed to Ghiberti by his patrons not only shows how highly they regarded him, but also reflects the new prestige which, on the threshold of the Renaissance, an artist could command.

The narrative cycle

Although the Door of Paradise was made later than the North door, in terms of sacred narrative it comes earlier, since its ten panels are devoted to the promise of salvation and the prophetic prefiguring of Christ in the Old Testament. The sequence proceeds from left to right and from top to bottom and presents, as we have seen, several biblical episodes in each panel. The first three stories – Adam and Eve (1), Cain and Abel (2), and Noah (3) – are followed by those which more explicitly illustrate God's saving role in the history of the Hebrew People, and the foreshadowing of the Messias: Abraham, the father of all believers, prepares to sacrifice the innocent Isaac, antetype of Christ (4); Esau selling his birthright to Jacob for a mess of pottage (5) symbolises the replacement of the Chosen People by the gentiles; Joseph, who forgives his brethren for having betrayed and sold him (6), is the image of Christ's sacrifice and mercy; the deeds of Moses (7), Josue (8) and David (9) emphasise the dependence of salvation on Divine intervention. The last panel, representing the encounter between Solomon and the Queen of Sheba (10), may be interpreted both as a symbol of the mystic marriage between Christ and his Church, and as a specific reference to the Union of the Greek and the Latin churches, proclaimed at the Council of Florence (1439).

The decoration of the frames

The narrative density of the panels in relief is paralleled by that of the frame, decorated with no fewer than forty-eight

biblical characters and prophets; twenty-four of them are full figure, set inside aedicules, and twenty-four are portrait medallions. In the centre, above the first two registers of panels, Ghiberti has inserted his own portrait (below) on the left-hand door and that of his son Vittore on the right-hand one.

At present only copies are to be seen on the Baptistery's exterior (see below).

The restoration
The Door of Paradise remained in position for the admiration of visitors until the flood of 1966, when the waters of the Arno swept against it with irresistible violence. Six of the ten panels – those we see today in the Museum – were ripped out of the frame, and had later to be carefully replaced.

Before setting the door back in its place the restorers carried out an initial cleaning of all the surfaces. The action of atmospheric agents, aggravated by pollution, had however seriously damaged the bronze, and a layer of oxides had formed on the surface of the metal causing loss of gilding. It was therefore decided to have the entire door restored by the Opificio delle Pietre Dure in Florence. The first panels to be restored were those detached in the flood; in 1990, when the first four panels were already in restoration, the door was moved to the laboratory of the Opificio and a gilded bronze copy was substituted for it. Today (2000) the Museum displays six panels, which will soon be joined by two more; within the next ten years, when work on the frame is completed, it will be possible to see the entire door reassembled.

The copy of the door
To get an overall idea of Ghiberti's masterpiece we have to rely on the gilded bronze copy set up on the east side of the Baptistery. The casting – making use of moulds taken immediately after the second world war – was carried out at the Marinelli foundry, and the gilding was done by the Paris firm of Chardon & Fils. For this final phase of the work the galvanic process was used, because European work-safety regulations prohibit the traditional method of gilding, as used by Ghiberti, which produces poisonous mercury vapours. The Japanese corporation Sun Motoyama made a substantial contribution to the costs of restoration.

We leave the room by the balcony, and turning right we go down the stairs to the ground floor. On the left an arch leads into the covered courtyard.

17. The courtyard

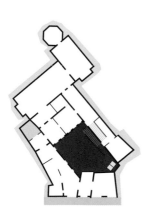

On the right, set into the wall above the old vestibule, is the 17th-century coat of arms of Cardinal Leopoldo de' Medici; at the sides are two *Agnus Dei*; in the centre is the monogram of the Opera; beneath is the half-obliterated motto *Videbunt iusti et laetabuntur* ("The just will see and rejoice").

On the left, backing onto a high marble wall (imitating the marble revetment of the Cathedral and of the Baptistery), we see a sculptural group that until recently surmounted the Door of Paradise, where it is now replaced by a copy. It is the BAPTISM OF CHRIST, commissioned in 1502 from Andrea Sansovino, who worked on it until 1505, when other commissions (first in Rome, then in Loreto) took him finally away from Florence. On the departure of the artist the ST JOHN was more or less finished, 1-3

Below, the *Baptism of Christ* by
ANDREA SANSOVINO and VINCENZO
DANTI, with the *Angel* by Innocenzo
Spinazzi. The original scheme
of Sansovino – not to be confused
with Jacopo Tatti, the pupil who
inherited his name – joined in
this group "a gently turning figure
(Christ) to a second (the Baptist)
whose body faces the viewer but
whose head is seen from the side"
(Giusti), renouncing the traditional
Angel and concentrating on the
other two instead. Andrea finished
only the *Baptist*; the *Christ* is for
the most part the work of Danti.

but the CHRIST had only been roughed out. After several
decades the commission to finish the group (with the addition of an angel) was awarded to Vincenzo Danti, a
sculptor from the circle of Michelangelo. By 1569 all that
remained to be done was to translate the plaster or stuc-
co model of the *Angel* into marble; however this had still
not been done when the sculptor died prematurely in
1576. The group was not completed until 1792, when Innocenzo Spinazzi sculpted the ANGEL we see today. As we
have seen (→ pp. 16-20), the commission awarded to
Sansovino was part of a scheme to replace the 14th-cen-
tury sculptures above the Baptistery doors with others
more suited to the taste of the times.

Above, a detail from the *Baptist* by Andrea Sansovino, in a photograph taken while the work was being restored at the Opificio delle Pietre Dure. During the Second World War the group was dismounted and carried to safety to avoid the dangers of bombardment; in the photographs of the time the statues still seem in good condition. In the summer of 1975, however, the right arm of the Christ, weakened at two points by acid rain, fell to the ground and shattered. It was then decided to restore the statues, which were replaced by copies made of plaster and marble dust.

We give here some technical information relating to Ghiberti's panels. Gilding is the process of applying a thin layer of gold to a surface. When gold leaf is applied to a surface the type of gilding is called *a foglia*. But most commonly-used procedures employ powdered gold: 'fire-gilding', in which the gold is dissolved in mercury which is then driven off by heating the resulting amalgam, and 'electro-plating', in which salts of gold are transformed by electrolysis into a thin film of precious oxide. In Ghiberti's panels (→ pp. 175-177) the layer of oxide which has formed over time between the bronze and the film of surface gold impinges on the gilding, but cannot be eliminated without removing the gilding itself; at present the panels are stabilised by being kept inside containers filled with nitrogen.

Opposite Sansovino's *Baptism of Christ* are the six restored PANELS from the ten which decorated the east door of the Baptistery, the so-called 'Door of Paradise' (→ pp. 174-177).

The glass containers which preserve them in nitrogen modify the incidence of natural light, and to some extent restrict our view of the reliefs; however, this is a necessary evil, because exposure to atmospheric oxygen and to variations in the level of humidity would undoubtedly ruin them.

Beginning with the panel nearest the door of the old vestibule, we see: the CREATION AND STORIES OF ADAM AND EVE; the STORIES OF JOSEPH; THE STORIES OF ESAU AND JACOB; the MEETING OF SOLOMON AND THE QUEEN OF SHEBA; the STORIES OF SAUL AND DAVID; the LABOURS OF ADAM AND EVE AND STORIES OF CAIN AND ABEL.   1-9

The two Roman sarcophagi which until the 1966 flood flanked the south door of the Baptistery will soon presumably be displayed in the courtyard (→ pp. 186-187).

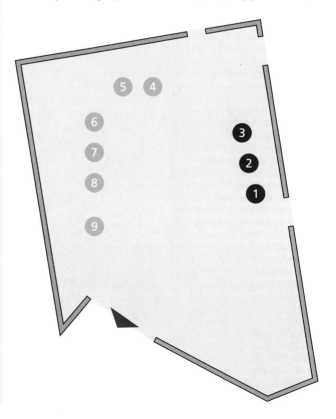

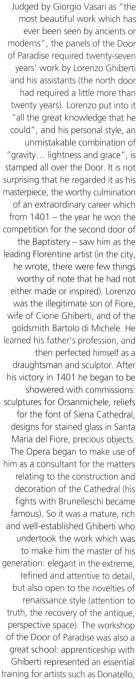

Judged by Giorgio Vasari as "the most beautiful work which has ever been seen by ancients or moderns", the panels of the Door of Paradise required twenty-seven years' work by Lorenzo Ghiberti and his assistants (the north door had required a little more than twenty years). Lorenzo put into it "all the great knowledge that he could", and his personal style, an unmistakable combination of "gravity… lightness and grace", is stamped all over the Door. It is not surprising that he regarded it as his masterpiece, the worthy culmination of an extraordinary career which from 1401 – the year he won the competition for the second door of the Baptistery – saw him as the leading Florentine artist (in the city, he wrote, there were few things worthy of note that he had not either made or inspired). Lorenzo was the illegitimate son of Fiore, wife of Cione Ghiberti, and of the goldsmith Bartolo di Michele. He learned his father's profession, and then perfected himself as a draughtsman and sculptor. After his victory in 1401 he began to be showered with commissions: sculptures for Orsanmichele, reliefs for the font of Siena Cathedral, designs for stained glass in Santa Maria del Fiore, precious objects. The Opera began to make use of him as a consultant for the matters relating to the construction and decoration of the Cathedral (his fights with Brunelleschi became famous). So it was a mature, rich and well-established Ghiberti who undertook the work which was to make him the master of his generation: elegant in the extreme, refined and attentive to detail, but also open to the novelties of renaissance style (attention to truth, the recovery of the antique, perspective space). The workshop of the Door of Paradise was also a great school: apprenticeship with Ghiberti represented an essential training for artists such as Donatello, Michelozzo and Luca della Robbia.

THE CREATION AND STORIES OF ADAM AND EVE

LABOURS OF ADAM AND EVE AND STORIES OF CAIN AND ABEL

Ghiberti replaced the gothic quatrefoil used in the existing doors (Andrea Pisano's and his own) and envisaged in Leonardo Bruni's original scheme (→ p. 174), with the large rectangles he had already adopted for the font of Siena Cathedral, where the narrative synthesis is obtained by perspective modulation of the relief. Each panel contains more than one episode: an innovation introduced by Sienese landscape painters of the 14th century, which Masaccio had used in the Brancacci Chapel. Here we give the scenes identified by Vasari in the panels reproduced on these two pages. In the *Stories of Adam and Eve* (opposite, above): the creation of Adam; the creation of Eve; the temptation; the expulsion. In the *Stories of Cain and Abel* (opposite, below): Adam and Eve with Cain and Abel; Cain and Abel offer first-fruits; Abel watches sheep while Cain ploughs the earth; Cain kills Abel; God questions Cain. In the *Stories of Esau and Jacob* (right, above): the birth of Esau and Jacob; Isaac salutes his son Esau setting out for the hunt; Rebecca and Jacob prepare to deceive Isaac with the skins of kids; Isaac blesses Jacob. In the *Stories of Joseph* (right, below): Joseph is cast by his brethren into the well; Joseph is sold to the merchants; the merchants consign him to Pharao; Joseph interprets Pharao's dream; Pharao pays him honour; Jacob sends his sons to Egypt for corn; Joseph recognises his brothers and returns to his father's house. Ghiberti really seems to improve from panel to panel, especially (says Vasari) "where there were houses". In the panel of the *Stories of Joseph* (right, below, "for all the effects and varieties of things… among all the works the most worthy and the most difficult and the most beautiful"), Lorenzo "made a round temple shown in perspective with great difficulty, inside which are figures in various attitudes loading corn and flour; and extraordinary donkeys".

STORIES OF ESAU AND JACOB

STORIES OF JOSEPH

The narrative scheme of the Door of Paradise synthesises some of the principal biblical stories, from Genesis to Kings. After the first panels concentrated on the theme of sin, the accent shifts to the subject of salvation by faith, and the prefiguring of the Redemption. The panels illustrating the stories of Noah, Moses, Josue and David were made in the 1440s. In the *Stories of Saul and David* (beside) we see David cutting off the head of Goliath "with a boyish and a proud attitude" (Vasari); the army of the Philistines is defeated, and David returns with the giant's severed head to his people, who welcome him rapturously. We have seen that in each panel Ghiberti adopts a different type of relief for each episode; in particular, in the far-off scenes and the backgrounds he makes use of the *stiacciato* technique invented by Donatello: this is a kind of very low relief in which the figures are distributed in a rigorous perspective space (a landscape or architecture) and which allows the artist to achieve an effect similar to that of a painting or drawing. The *Meeting between Solomon and the Queen of Sheba* (right), where there is a "house drawn in perspective, very beautiful", has often been seen as a direct reference to the Council of Florence (originally convoked at Ferrara, and moved to Florence by Pope Eugenius IV in 1439 at the request of Cosimo the Elder), whose purpose was to reunite the Latin and Greek Churches. In the door, writes Vasari, "one realises what the skill and genius of a sculptor can do when he is casting figures in the round, in half relief, in low relief, or in very low relief. In the composition, the striking poses of his male and female figures, in the variety of the architectural perspectives, and the consistently graceful bearing of both sexes, he demonstrated his grasp of decorum, expressing gravity in the old, and lightness and grace in the young".

STORIES OF SAUL AND DAVID

THE MEETING OF SOLOMON AND THE QUEEN OF SHEBA

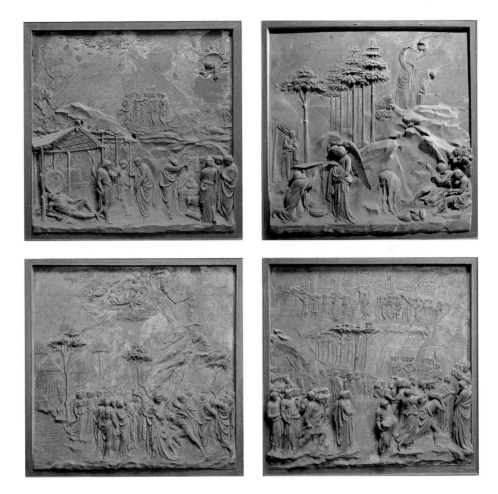

Above (from top left), the panels with the scenes of *Noah*, *Abraham*, *Moses* and *Josue*, still in restoration at the Opificio. The words of Vasari on this last panel well illustrate Ghiberti's technique: "very beautiful are some [figures] in low relief, when the ark is carried around the walls of the city… with the sound of the trumpet the walls fall and the Hebrews capture Jericho; in which the landscape is diminished, and lowered with observation of the first figures to the mountains, and from the mountains to the city, and finally from the city to the far distance in very low relief".

As we go out, we notice on the left wall of the passage two plaques.

The upper one, placed on 23 June 1902, commemorates Luigi Del Moro, the pupil of Emilio De Fabris who designed the Museum and completed the new façade of the Cathedral. The lower one records the founding of the Museum: "having found again, through the diligence of the architect Emilio De Fabris, the supports of the choirs made by Luca della Robbia and Donatello and having recovered the figurative portions through the unfailing efforts of the deputies… the secular delegation of S. Maria del Fiore had this Museum built… in order to display those marvellous works of art now restored to their original state and the subject of universal admiration".

The Roman sarcophagi

Originally the space between the Baptistery and the old cathedral of Santa Reparata (which was demolished to make room for Santa Maria del Fiore) was occupied by a cemetery. As well as ordinary graves there were a great many Roman sarcophagi, witnesses to the close relations between Rome and *Florentia* during the later centuries of the Empire and the early Middle Ages: many of these artefacts – which were produced at Rome in almost industrial quantities – were sent out to the provinces for use not only as tombs but also purely as ornaments. Over the centuries even those carved with pagan scenes ended up in Christian cemeteries, 'recycled' as tombs for nobles.

A most interesting recollection of their presence has been left to us by Giovanni Boccaccio in a short novella, little more than an anecdote, narrated in the *Decameron* (VI, 9). The scene is set in the later 13th century, when groups of young Florentine nobles formed themselves into bands, and used to ride through the streets of the city and hold banquets. The leader of one of these bands, Betto Brunelleschi, longed to have as one of his companions the poet Guido Cavalcanti, who was famous for his wit, his noble accomplishments and his riches. But the scholarly Guido always refused, since he had nothing in common with Betto's friends except his noble birth. Reluctant to admit that they were being rejected for their human qualities, Betto's band decided that Guido, a "natural philosopher" suspected of atheism, was too preoccupied with weighty intellectual matters.

One day it happened that Guido Cavalcanti was walking by himself in Piazza Santa Reparata (the name given to the area between the Baptistery and the first cathedral), wandering among the "great marble tombs", when Betto's band came galloping towards him, crying "Here you are, refusing to join our band. When you've found out that

God does not exist, where will that have got you?".

Putting his "hand on a tomb (they were not small), he answered: 'Seeing that here you are at home, my lords, you can say to me what you please', and with that vaulted over the tomb most athletically, and vanished from their sight". They were all astonished at his words, until Betto explained to his companions what Guido had meant: the sarcophagi are the homes of the dead; plain unlettered dunces are no better than dead men compared with learned people like him.

All that remains of those "great marble tombs" today is a pair of Roman sarcophagi of the 2nd-3rd century AD, which until 1966 stood either side of the south door of the Baptistery; their presence there is documented since the 14th century. After the flood the sarcophagi were cleaned and placed in the courtyard of the Museum until 1998, when they were carefully restored in the laboratory of the Opera.

The first has its front divided into three niches. The central one is surmounted by a triangular pediment supported by twisted columns and shows the joining of right hands (*dextrarum iunctio*), the symbolic action of a Roman wedding equivalent to our exchange of rings. The groom wears a toga, and the bride has her head covered by the red nuptial veil (*flammeum*). In the intercolumnar spaces between the central niche and the lateral ones we see the same couple, now separated in death. The wife is dressed in the pallium and stole, the typical garments of a Roman matron; the husband, evidently a soldier, is in military garb, consisting of a lorica and mantle. The lateral niches, with rounded pediments, contain Castor and Pollux, the two demi-gods who guide souls into the next world.

Of the two sides, the right shows a *victimarius* (the priest's assistant, whose duty is to immolate the victims) leading an ox, and the left a barbarian captive brought before the *imperator* or commander. The lid is worked with fictive tiles in the shape of laurel leaves.

In the second sarcophagus (opposite page) – the lid of which disappeared after the 1966 flood – the columns are replaced by pilaster strips. In the centre is a doorway, also surmounted by a triangular pediment; through its half-closed doors emerges Mercury, another 'psychopompus' or leader of souls to Elysium. In the narrow spaces between the pilasters are two diminutive winged Victories, bearing the emblems of the deceased's military (right) and civic (left) virtues. The lateral niches contain images of the spouses: the man, wearing a toga, is flanked by a child and by a container with papyrus rolls, indicative of some sort of scholarly activity; beside the wife (above), who is again dressed in pallium and stole, there is a peacock, sacred to Juno, and a flower (both are symbols of love and of conjugal fidelity). The sides have bas-reliefs of gryphons: they are not creatures of classical mythology, and their presence demonstrates the powerful influence exercised by oriental cults in late imperial times.

Index of artists

Bibliographical Note

Among the older sources, see, in addition to the *Divine Comedy* by DANTE ALIGHIERI and the *Decameron* by GIOVANNI BOCCACCIO, the *Chronicles* of GIOVANNI VILLANI (for a selection of this work see *Cronica, con le continuazioni di Matteo e Filippo*, ed. by G. Aquilecchia, Torino, Einaudi, 1979); the *Commentaries* of LORENZO GHIBERTI (*I commentarii...*, ed. by L. Bartoli, Firenze, Giunti, 1998); the biographical works of ANTONIO MANETTI (for an English translation, see *The life of Brunelleschi*, ed. by H. Saalman, transl. by C. Enggass, University Park Pa., Pennsylvania State UP, 1970), ASCANIO CONDIVI (for an English translation, see *Michelangelo. Life, letters, and poetry*, ed. by G. Bull, Oxford-New York, Oxford UP, 1999) and GIORGIO VASARI: both editions of the *Vite* (1550 and 1568) are edited by R. Bettarini, Firenze, Sansoni, 1966-1988; for English translations, see *The lives of the artists*, ed. by J. Conaway Bondanella and P. Bondanella, Oxford-New York, Oxford UP, 1991; *Lives of the artists*, a selection transl. by G. Bull, Harmondsworth, Penguin, 1987.

For the Museum's collection, the catalogue by LUISA BECHERUCCI and GIULIA BRUNETTI, *Il Museo dell'Opera del Duomo di Firenze,* Milano-Firenze, Electa, 1969-1970 (2 vols.), is still fundamental. Other catalogues and guides, quite apart from their quality, are to be regarded as superseded on account of the new acquisitions and the new arrangement. Still indispensable are the documentary collections by CESARE GUASTI (*La cupola di Santa Maria del Fiore, illustrata con i documenti di Archivio dell'Opera secolare*, Firenze, Barbera Bianchi, 1857; *Santa Maria del Fiore. La costruzione della chiesa e del campanile*, photographic reprint of the 1887 edition, Bologna, Forni, 1974) and GIOVANNI POGGI (*Il Duomo di Firenze. Documenti sulla decorazione della chiesa e del campanile tratti dall'Archivio dell'Opera*, ed. by M. Haines, Firenze, Medicea-Kunsthistorisches Institut, 1989, the first volume of which is a photographic reprint of the 1909 Berlin edi-

tion). For the history of the institution see M. HAINES, "L'Arte della Lana e l'Opera del Duomo di Firenze, con un accenno a Ghiberti tra due istituzioni", in *Opera. Carattere e ruolo delle fabbriche cittadine fino all'inizio dell'età moderna*, proceedings of the Colloquium (Florence, Villa I Tatti, 3 April 1991), ed. by M. HAINES and L. RICETTI, Firenze, Olschki, 1996; *La cattedrale e la città* and *La cattedrale come spazio sacro*, ed. by T. VERDON and A. INNOCENTI, Firenze, EDIFIR, 2000. See also *Due granduchi, tre re e una facciata*, exhibition catalogue (Florence, 2 June-8 September 1987), Firenze, Alinea, 1987; *I libri del Duomo di Firenze. Codici liturgici e Biblioteca di Santa Maria del Fiore (secoli XI-XVI)*, exhibition catalogue (Florence, 23 September 1997-10 January 1998), ed. by L. FABBRI and M. TACCONI, Firenze, Centro Di, 1997; *Sotto il cielo della Cupola. Il coro di Santa Maria del Fiore dal Rinascimento al 2000...*, exhibition catalogue (Florence, 18 June-21 September 1997), Milano, Electa, 1997.

There is a vast bibliography on the cathedral complex and the artists involved in its construction and decoration. For these works see the apparatus in the catalogue by Becherucci and Brunetti, as well as in publications accessible to the wider public, including the interesting recent series "Alla riscoperta di Piazza del Duomo in Firenze", edited by TIMOTHY VERDON (Firenze, Centro Di, 1992-1998); *Il Battistero di San Giovanni a Firenze/The Baptistery of San Giovanni, Florence*, ed. by A. PAOLUCCI, Modena, Franco Cosimo Panini, 1994 (2 vols.); F. GURRIERI, C. ACIDINI LUCHINAT et al., *La cattedrale di Santa Maria del Fiore a Firenze*, Firenze, Giunti-Cassa di Risparmio, 1994-1995 (2 vols.).

Among publications by Mandragora we would mention A. BICCHI-A. CIANDELLA, *Testimonia Sanctitatis. Le reliquie e i reliquiari del Duomo e del Battistero*, Firenze 1999, and A. GIUSTI, *The Baptistery of San Giovanni in Florence*, Firenze 2000. Shortly to be published, G. FANELLI-M. FANELLI, *The Cupola of Brunelleschi*; A. BICCHI-A. CIANDELLA, *I paramenti sacri della cattedrale di Santa Maria del Fiore*; G. DI CAGNO, *The Cathedral, the Baptistery and the Campanile*, 2nd revised and enlarged edition.

Table of Contents

Printed by Alpilito - Firenze
November 2000